Y0-EHY-116

LIBRARY - COLLEGE USA

BOOKS BY LOUIS SHORES

1934 ORIGINS OF THE AMERICAN COLLEGE LIBRARY
1936 BIBLIOGRAPHIES AND SUMMARIES IN EDUCATION (with W. S. Monroe)
1937 BASIC REFERENCE BOOKS
1939 BASIC REFERENCE BOOKS; Revised
1947 HIGHWAYS IN THE SKY
1950 GENERAL EDUCATION (with W. H. Stickler and J. P. Stoakes)
1953 CHALLENGES TO LIBRARIANSHIP
1954 BASIC REFERENCE SOURCES
1960 INSTRUCTIONAL MATERIALS
1965 MARK HOPKINS' LOG
1966 THE LIBRARY-COLLEGE (with Robert Jordan and John Harvey)
1967 AROUND THE LIBRARY WORLD IN 76 DAYS
1968 THE TEX-TEC SYLLABI (with Mayrelee Newman, Richard T. Wilkinson, *et al*)

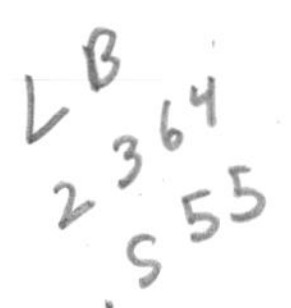

LIBRARY - COLLEGE USA:

Essays On a Prototype for an American Higher Education

By
Louis Shores

Tallahassee, Florida
South Pass Press
1970

Out of concern
for current campus unrest,
I dedicate this book, to the
GENERATIONS TOGETHER —
Faculty and Students
Who prefer to communicate intellectually,
Rather than physically,
And who are quietly, but positively,
Experimenting and innovating
With the prototypes
For tomorrow's Higher Education.

CONTENTS

PREFACE

THIRTY-SIX YEARS ago I read a paper at the Chicago World's Fair convention of the American Library Association. It was titled, "The Library Arts College, A Possibility in 1954?" It reflected my own undergraduate revolt against the American higher educational establishment. Principally I dissented with the classroom-centered learning mode; with the meaning of "liberal" as fortified by a curriculum hierarchy of predatory disciplines; with the library's "ancillary" role in the preparation of the next generation. There were other dissatisfactions, too, which I enumerated subsequently. But, the identification of problems, despite my respect for the scientific method, has always excited me less than the discovery of solutions. The "Library Arts College" was my 1934 essay.

First published in *School and Society,* and subsequently republished several times, "The Library Arts College" is presented, toward the end of this volume, once more. Robert Jordan has cited this essay as the beginning of the Library-College movement in the United States. I make no claims for originating the idea. My inspiration came first, probably, from my reading of Thomas Carlyle's *Heroes and Hero Worship*. It came next from my early decision to devote my life to librarianship. Along the way I became fascinated by the encyclopedia, and discovered in its concept of summarizing all of the knowledge significant to mankind a new dimension in learning. In this very idea of summarization I discovered the mundane technique of getting better grades in college by always reading for overview in all of the subjects for which I planned to enroll the next term. Putting these things together with some of my other discoveries and frustrations I came up with an ideal college I should like to develop some day. I sketched "The Library Arts College," forerunner of the current Library-College.

LIBRARY-COLLEGE USA

When a college is a library and a library is a college it is a Library-College. (Note that the term is always spelled with a hyphen.) The Library-College is a very special kind of college, and a very special kind of library. Its college individuality is in its *learning mode.* The uniqueness of its library is in the concept of the *Generic Book.* If these two distinctions are mentioned first, it is only because understandings of them are a prelude to the presentation of my kind of Library-College.

The Library-College *learning mode* reverses the traditional relationship of classroom-library to library-classroom. Instead of going to classes regularly, and visiting the library irregularly, as time permits, the Library-College I favor advocates regular, student independent study in the library, at his individual workbench, we call a carrel; "wet," if possible, or as "damp" as finances and technology will permit. (At this very beginning, let it be understood, there is not unanimous agreement among us on details in the movement.) Under faculty bibliographic guidance, the student proceeds as far as he can on his own, first; then in dialogue with fellow students; next in conference with faculty; finally in seminar, classroom, laboratory, lecture, etc.

In this learning mode the faculty role is almost as reversed as is the student's. Instead of meeting a class at regular hours, the instructors hold irregular class or group meetings as the occasion demands or suggests. For example, conference hours are regular, and a most significant part of the faculty work day. Seminars, labs, classes take on a new significance because they result from student need for elaboration of a point, or reconciliation of conflicting concepts. The lecture resumes its creative position in the learning mode, with each faculty member preparing an original presentation on a specialty not comparably covered in any other medium.

But the high art of the college teacher becomes the sensitive matching of individual differences in his students with individual differences in media. To perform bibliographically in this way college faculty must know books and libraries better than they have in the past. In 1940, Chancellor Harvie Branscomb, in his classic *Teaching With Books* (a study of library impact on American higher education, undertaken for the Association of American Colleges, and financed by the Carnegie Corporation) revealed how inadequately college faculties used books and libraries in their teaching. The Library-College learning mode demands of the new breed of faculty a knowledge of books and libraries that goes even beyond the understandings of traditional librarianship.

Which brings us to the difference in the concept of Library for the Library-College. Every academic library in the United States, today, probably, when it speaks of book selection, means *printed* book selection. If the library includes materials that are called "audiovisual," such materials are referred to as "non-book." This is contrary to the concept of a Library-College Library, which is concerned with *generic book selection.* I first indicated my own concept of the *Generic Book* in my editorial for the *Saturday Review* in 1958, on the occasion of the first National Library Week.

Briefly, the *Generic Book,* can be defined as *the sum total of man's communication possibilities.* It includes all media *formats, subjects,* and *levels.* Under this definition, a 16 mm motion picture is just as much of a book as, for example, a collection of 32 or more pages of paper, bound or loose-leaf, consisting of printed reading matter or illustrations (to condense a 1943 U. S. War Production Board limitation order, January L-245) . Other formats of the *Generic Book* include, filmstrips, and transparencies; discs, tapes, radio transcriptions and videotapes; community resources—natural, social, human; programmed materials print, machine, and computer-assisted, as well as all kinds of print, and other sensory, and even extra-sensory media, all of which I have enumerated in other writings that describe my format classification of the *Generic Book.*

Why the *Generic Book* is integral to Library-College library book selection, and to the Library-College learning mode, is because for the first time in the history of education media are so plentiful, and so varied in format, subject, and level, that individual differences in students can be matched by individual differences in media. And the format variation is particularly significant to learning. In all the furor about Marshall McLuhan's "massage," there is really only one point: the format of the medium may affect communicability, and therefore learning, in the case of Educational Media. The Library-College takes advantage of this phenomenon.

The Library-College recognizes the fact that one learner may learn better a particular fact, principle, or theory from a printed page; another student from a time-lapse motion picture; a third from a videotape; a fourth from a transparency overlay. Nor does it forget the level of maturity of the student, with which librarians and teachers have long been concerned. And, of course, the librarian through his classification systems has been as conscious of subjects as has his classroom faculty colleagues operating under the strict discipline boundaries of curricula and learned societies. Consequently, Library-College library book selection is three-prong: subject, level, format, throughout.

Perhaps this is enough for an opener, which is part of what a preface can be. Another part usually points out what is to follow. I have gathered together many of my shorter writings relating to the Library-College, dating back to that opening essay in 1934. The arrangement is one that appealed to me. Part one aims to present the idea in general. Since the Junior College movement has in many ways paralleled and offered some reinforcements I have devoted considerable attention to this division of academic librarianship. Hence part two. And then I have been concerned about the essential components—faculty, librarian, library, student, professional education. These essays have been placed in part three. What I call foundations are in my original 1934 effort, in the Jamestown College Charter, and in the outline for my Library-College, prepared for the Jamestown conference. That is part four.

Finally, every author as he writes his preface, particularly, wonders what kind of reception his book will get. He trembles some about the ambusher ready to shoot down errors in form, format, fact. Every encyclopedist knows the type of review that can catalogue 500 errors in 500,000 facts, which first brought recognition to S. S. Van Dine under his real name of Willard Huntington Wright. These kinds of editorial errors are probably here. They are my fault.

But I beg of you to look at the idea of the Library-College, above all. I believe the trend to independent study in our colleges offers libraries and librarianship a new opportunity. That opportunity is to design a prototype for the higher education of tomorrow that will more nearly meet the needs of our youth.

October 31, 1969. Louis Shores

LIBRARY-COLLEGE USA

PART ONE: THE IDEA

1.

"The inevitable culmination of the independent study movement . . ."

THE LIBRARY-COLLEGE IDEA

(An article written especially for the *Library Journal*, 1966, 91:3871-75)

WHEN A COLLEGE is a library and a library is a college, it is a Library College.

Something like that is about to happen at Jamestown College, North Dakota. Five days before last Christmas, some two dozen Library collegers gathered to design a bold new experiment for a nation and an age committed to higher education for all of the people. In the gathering were college presidents, deans, professors, librarians, and representatives of foundations and governments. After four days of deliberation an idea for a Library-College emerged.

The Library-College is the inevitable culmination of the independent study movement. Call it honors reading, or by such variations on the theme as autonomous courses at Antioch, or preceptorial or tutorial plans at Princeton and Harvard, respectively, the essence of the learning mode is independent study at the individual's pace, in the library, rather than group teaching at an "average" rate in the classroom. To this point, independent study has been, largely, the prerogative of the superior student. The Library-College proposes to make independent study the rule for all students regardless of their range of talents.

With America's commitment to universal higher education, the range of individual differences in the student population promises to be wider than ever before in the history of higher education. These differences are becoming increasingly difficult to meet through the traditional group approach of the classroom. College students in mounting numbers are revolting against the lockstep of class room contact as a measure of education. In recent surveys of college student opinion, the most often repeated criticism has been of the growing impersonality of education. Students declared: "I don't get much out of class. If they would just turn me loose in the library I believe I could learn much more about any subject, almost."

In the spring of 1964, 11 experimenting colleges described their innovations at Wakulla Springs in a unique seminar sponsored by Florida State University.[1] At the heart of all of these innovations in higher education is independent study in the library as the learning mode. One of the experimenting colleges, Florida Presbyterian, suspends all classes during each January for total student independent study in the library. Comparable reading accents are described in the college programs at Antioch, Stephens, Monteith, Parsons.

Other evidences of the growing trend to independent study in US higher education can be found in the rash of honors reading programs that have broken out on new and old campuses. Harvard Medical School has recently acceded to a student rebellion against classroom lectures by authorizing independent individual study. Independent study as an evidence of higher education has indeed been recognized as cardinal by the much quoted and stimulating US Office of Education "New Dimensions" pamphlet by Winslow Hatch.[2]

When the Library-College idea was first proposed is uncertain. Robert Jordan of the Council of Library Resources, a leader in the movement, has generously suggested[3] that my paper, "The Library Arts College," read before the American Library Association's Chicago World's Fair Convention in 1933, and subsequently printed and reprinted by *School and Society*, was the beginning of the movement.[4] But I acknowledge my own inspiration from Thomas Carlyle's essay "The Hero as Intellectual," from which comes the often quoted line, out of context, "The true university is a collection of books."[5] In the years since World War II, the influence of the British universities, which I had the opportunity to observe first hand during my Fulbright year, has confirmed the superiority of reading in a subject to attending classes.

Elements of the Library-College idea have appeared in various US colleges. Notable was the innovation of the Stephens College "vitalized" concept,[6] which combined the positions of librarian and dean of the college in the same person. Dr. B. Lamar Johnson, the Stephens innovator, is one of the Jamestown consultants. Another Jamestown consultant, Patricia Knapp, has done much along the Library-College way at Monteith. The new University of California at Santa Cruz has announced, even before opening, that its cluster of small colleges "will make more than usual use of independent study . . ." and "The library will be the intellectual heart of the Santa Cruz campus. . . ."[7]

Antioch, where "Independent study has been open to students since the reorganized program of 1921 . . ." has now under consideration "an experimental program for the freshman year which, if adopted by the faculty, will incorporate independent study techniques into the entire program from the first year on."[8] At Parsons, the time had come to shift the emphasis "from training and informing our students to putting a great deal of weight on the process of making them think or educating them. . . . To this end (writes the librarian) I conducted a campaign among faculty and administration that resulted in a program that was more than I had asked for. All upper division courses and selected courses in the core were to have term papers or equivalent library projects."[9]

At Florida Presbyterian, "The Winter term is a special four to five week period of independent study for all undergraduates. . . . Designed to develop the qualities of self-discipline in pursuits requiring the student to be the prime explorer, the winter term asks him to work without customary routine of classroom and lecture hall on a single problem. . . . With guidance he elaborates and limits his subject, gathers material, organizes it and presents it as a paper, a short story, a painting, a piece of laboratory equipment. . . . Throughout the four weeks, the professor is available for consultation and guidance, and each student is expected to put in weekly 50 to 60 hours of study."[10]

Much more evidence of the impact of this independent study trend upon higher education in America could be related. In recent months, at least two junior colleges have indicated an interest in the "library junior college" described in *Junior College Journal*.[11] Several college presidents have requested information on elements of the senior library college.[12] In 1963, the first of a series of talkshops on the library college idea was held at Kenyon College in Ohio; a second was held at Florida State; and a third at Syracuse University. A fourth is now in the planning stage. The Jamestown College meeting appears to be the first total commitment to the idea by an American institution of higher education. Under President Dan Sillers' dynamic leadership, faculty and students are excitedly exploring an adventure in liberal education which will be reported in a forthcoming volume.[13]

Impact of the independent study trend on academic librarianship has only begun to be felt. Except for the small group of librarians involved in the Jamestown experiment, and the slightly larger group receiving and contributing to the *Library College News Letter*,[14] honors reading and other variations of the independent study trend have thus far only stimulated college librarians to accelerate traditional efforts. For the most part, independent study has stirred librarians to improve faculty book selection, and to seek short cuts to better acquisition, processing, and circulation of materials, enlisting wherever possible hardware automation. These efforts have been desirable in many instances, but in all cases they have represented the ancillary, retrieval concept of the role of librarianship in the learning process.

But the independent study trend is confronting academic librarianship with the prospect that soon there will be no classroom instruction to support. In the past, we have celebrated our subordination to what instructors do in scheduled class meetings. With the passing of the classroom as the center of learning, the college librarian can persist in his ancillary role of retrieving books ever more vigorously, and perhaps electronically—*or*, he can at last assume his initiatory position in the learning process, recognizing that he is better equipped to guide the undergraduate to a liberal education in the library than are most of his colleagues who try to teach in the classroom.

The librarian's better equipment for the learning process stems basically from his superior knowledge of library resources. For the first time in the history of education, the quantity, variety, and range of the generic book matches individual differences found in students. Considered from the standpoint of subject, level, or format, it is now possible to select a medium of communication that will subtly and delicately contribute to an individual learning situation. Because of this fact, tailored, individual, independent study offers a revolutionary approach to learning. But fundamental to such a concept of education is a mastery of library resources—and the average classroom instructor has this to a smaller degree than the average librarian.

High above our old library building, the quotation from that versatile author *Anon.* is still visible and true: "The half of knowledge is knowing where to find it." And this half the librarian knows better than any colleague on the faculty. The first action on the part of our profession, therefore, in this independent study movement, is to revitalize our instruction in library use. Even the best of our orientation weeks and freshman courses of the present and past hardly prepare our undergraduates in this "half." In the Library-College, instruction in resources encompasses the whole range of media, from textbook to television, from hard cover to computer console, from graphic to tape, from projection to programmed machine. It calls for the kind of "sophistication in the use of the University's library (in the words of the Dean of Monteith, paying tribute to Pat Knapp) such as I have never seen before. . . ."[15] To achieve this sophistication in the "half of knowledge," librarianship must come up with a new dimension in teaching library use, and education must allocate unprecedented curriculum prominence to this subject. In at least one concept of the Library-College curriculum, one half of the first term's academic time is devoted to a study of this half of knowledge.

As for the other half, of both knowledge and the first term, the librarian is again better equipped than most of his classroom teaching colleagues. Concern over increasing specialism early and late in the undergraduate program led, shortly after the last World War, to several so-called integrated areas in the general education of the first two college years. In place of separate math, physics, and chemistry courses, for example, an area course in the physical sciences was introduced. Similarly, separate courses in botany, zoology, physiology gave way to a single course in "bi sci"; sociology, political science, and economics courses merged into a broad social science offering; and the previous individual philosophy, religion, fine arts, and literature classes became an overview humanities course. The Library-College suggests an even further integration in the form of beginning and capstone inter-disciplinary approaches to knowledge.

The extreme commitment of our classroom faculties to predatory subject specializations often confronts the undergraduate with a universe in which God is a chemist every Monday, Wednesday, Friday morning from eight to ten; an economist Tuesday and Thursday from three to five; a Greek classicist at three other hours during the week. Only in the library is the unity of knowledge restored. There, the librarian with fairness and objectivity usually tries to serve impartially all of the so-called disciplines. Further, some of the more imaginative librarians have occasionally had the brashness to fill the interdiscipline interstices for the student. Indeed, many a student has first learned the satisfaction of serendipity, a term only lately rediscovered by science, in the library with a librarian who dared to consider himself the teaching equal of a classroom instructor.

Because of this concern with the interdisciplines, this traditional commitment to generalism in a world of specialisms, the librarian better than any other member of the faculty is equipped to teach the *gestalt* of the other half of knowledge; to carry off the responsibility of the second half of the first academic term. As some designers of the Library-College see it, these generalia areas of the curriculum, coming at the beginning and at the end of the undergraduate program, provide balance and perspective to the intervening terms of increasing specialism. Thus the curriculum of the first term of the Library-College suggests two foundational courses, one dealing with the half of knowledge that covers knowing where to find it, that is, sources; and the other offering an encyclopedic summary of the knowledge most significant to mankind. For instruction in both these areas no faculty member is better equipped that the librarian who will commit himself to this new role.

That is not to say that the librarian cannot also teach (via the library) any of the subject specialisms. We now have librarians with doctorates, research, and teaching experience in nearly all of the disciplines. They can, if they will, reform the classroom teaching mode of the past into a vital, library independent study education that will more nearly relate to the needs and talents of the individual.

Fundamental to the success of the Library-College is a new

generation of college faculty. The embryo can be found today in the classroom instructors who teach with books; and in the librarians who put library instruction above management. Inevitably, the new breed will be a cross between these two groups, and those who persist in medieval oral communication to groups in classrooms, no less than those who insist that the high role of librarianship is organization for retrieval, will be forced to fight for faculty status.

The signs are unmistakable. In the independent study trend are the beginnings of a new education. In these same trends there are irresistible inducements to prepare the next generation of classroom and library faculty to merge their talents to create the coming Library-College.

REFERENCES

1. Stickler, W. H. *Experimental Colleges*. 1964. 185pp.
2. Hatch, Winslow. *What Standards Do We Raise?* US Office of Education, 1963. (New Dimensions in Higher Education, No. 12)
3. Jordan, Robert. "The Library College: a Merging of Library and Classroom." *The Library College*, 1966.
4. Shores, Louis. "The Library Arts College." *School and Society*, 1935. Vol. 41, pp. 110-14.
5. Carlyle, Thomas. "The Hero as Intellectual." *Heroes and Hero Worship*, 1848.
6. Johnson, B. L. *Vitalizing a College Library*, 1939. 122pp.
7. McHenry, Dean E. "The University of California, Santa Cruz." *Experimental Colleges*, 1964, pp. 138, 141-2.
8. Oldt, Esther A. "Antioch College as an Experimental Institution." *Experimental Colleges*, 1964, p. 28.
9. Sutton, Lee. "Parsons College: Experiment as the Art of the Possible." *Experimental Colleges*, 1964, pp. 66-67.
10. Bevan, J. M. "Florida Presbyterian College: New Adventure in Education." *Experimental Colleges*, 1964, p. 96.
11. Shores, Louis. "The Library Junior College." *Junior College Journal*, 1966. Vol 36, pp. 6-9.
12. Shores, Louis. "The True University," *Alabama Librarian*, 1965. Vol. 17, pp. 13-18.
13. Shores, Louis, and Jordan, Robert. *The Library College*. Drexel Institute Press, 1966 (in press).
14. Jordan, Robert. *The Library College News-Letter*. 1965-66 (Nos. 1-4).
15. Ross, W. O. "Monteith College of Wayne State University." *Experimental Colleges*, 1964, p. 149.

2.

ALONG THE LIBRARY-COLLEGE WAY

(An essay for the opening faculty meeting, Elmira College, Elmira, N. Y., September, 1967. Elmira is the oldest woman's college in the United States, hence the use of the feminine pronoun. Published *Peabody Journal of Education,* 1968, 46:165-176)

INNOVATION COMPULSION is a feeling that somehow intoxicates all of us who have given our lives to the higher education of young people. Historically we cannot help being stirred by this new, magnificent first, our United States is attempting. While much of the world is still striving to overcome illiteracy with elementary schools, and most of the world does not yet have compulsory secondary schooling, our nation is boldly moving to college for all.

Philosophically I believe in this. Whether or not I can prove it by the hallowed scientific method, there is some evidence in history that revolutions are caused, partially at least, when leaders and followers can no longer communicate with each other. Universal higher education I consider the best insurance against violence in change. And in these days of increasing urban disturbances almost any policy of promise is worthy of the investment.

But college for all involves some reformation that includes intellectual, if not physical turbulence. I refer not alone to the growing student unrest, especially on the campuses of our multiuniversities, but to increasing faculty concern with teaching, as we have practiced it, gladly and sadly, over the centuries. Much of this concern emanates from the two so-called "explosions" of population and information that are now a "must" in any commencement oration.

For us, I contend the student population increase is a more serious challenge than the geometric swarms of facts being exposed daily. When the multiversity president responded facetiously the other day to the question, "How many students do you now have" with "Oh, about 10%," he was phenomenally observing that we who teach are now dealing with a wider range of individual differences in our classrooms than higher education has ever known before. Yet we are largely continuing our group instruction approach, which must necessarily be aimed at an increasingly unrepresentative average. Inevitably not only the gifted and the dropout are being neglected, but a greater portion of those who comprise the majority of the bell-shaped curve.

Repeated polls of student discontent reported by our newspapers and magazines reveal, at the very top, resentment of the growing impersonality caused by numbers, and the lockstep of classroom instruction. There are other dissents with higher educational practices in America, of course: the curriculum, for example, but especially with the class contact as a basic measure of learning.

FACULTY INNOVATION

Before another educational layman makes a cover photo in *Time* or *Newsweek*, let us make it abundantly clear that the learning of our young people has been of longer and deeper concern to the faculties of American colleges and universities than to anyone. Most of the criticism of education that make headlines, as well as the panaceas, have been tried, tested, developed or rejected by us. If these pedagogues will take the trouble to study the professional literature of only the last few years, these critics will discover educational experimenting all over this land. They will, indeed, be amazed at the number of conferences of educators, philanthropists, parents, students, and government, business, and professional leaders that have been devoted to the subject of educational change.

If I cite only four, it is because I have been deeply involved in them. In the fourth quarter of an FSU-Houston football game in 1960, three deans departed reluctantly for the airport to rendezvous with a Southern Association evaluating team scheduled to rehearse the next day in Lubbock, Texas. Enroute to the Texas Tech visitation, the dean of the College of Arts and Sciences, the Dean of Students, and the Dean of the Graduate Library School, excitedly talked about starting an experimental college at Florida State University, that would go beyond anything Glenn Frank at Wisconsin had considered many years before.

ALONG THE LIBRARY-COLLEGE WAY

The great conversation began aboard a National airliner, continued during sight seeing at a New Orleans stopover, and right up to that Texas rehearsal. When we returned to campus, we invited three more to join us—the graduate school dean, the library director, the chairman of our department of higher education in the School of Education. For a year and a half we met one night a week in each of our homes, rotating location regularly, so that each wife would have a chance at preparing the midnight snacks that followed the design discussions for our prototype college.

Our concerns were first with the growing impersonality resulting from skyrocketing enrollments. We have been Florida State College for Women for forty years, following chartering as a men's college, and conversion in the third decation to coeducation. When I arrived on the campus in 1946, the Buckman Act, which had taken the men away from the campus, had just been repealed. In the years that followed, enrollment climbed from under 1,000 to over 14,000. Every registration day there was a mob scene in the gymnasium, designed to discourage all but the stout-hearted. From that point on, the ID number, and the computer took over. Class attendance, three times a week for about 15 weeks, put three semester hours of credit in the academic bank book. There was also the additional gimmick of quality points. Something called a Retention Table was carried about, fearfully, by every student. Out there somewhere, was the robot that might drop a blue IBM card into your mailbox at the end of the term, with only the two curt words, "Academic Dismissal."

These were only symbols of our discontent with the academic climate. Our dissatisfactions ranged from the classroom lockstep to the compartmentalized curriculum; from the segregated and inadequate student counselling, to the cumulation of credits as an evidence of education. Above all, we wanted to restore the student as an individual; to fire his intellectual concern; to revitalize faculty-student communication in their common goal of continuous learning.

After we had broadly sketched our design for the prototype experimental college, it occurred to us that we would like to share with other experimenting colleges and universities. With aid from the Southern Regional Education Board, we sponsored the Wakulla Springs Colloquium in the spring of 1963. The volume *Experi-*

mental Colleges describes eleven innovational efforts on campuses in all parts of the United States.

Although the Wakulla reports accent independent study, along the way to the Library-College, none of the eleven institutions can be fairly identified as examples of the concept. But in December 1966 one college, Jamestown in North Dakota, invited some thirty college presidents, deans, professors, representatives of government agencies and foundations to explore the Library-College idea found in the volume *The Library-College*. Among other documents, the Jamestown Charter is significant for its definition:

> The purpose of the Library-College is to increase the effectiveness of student learning, particularly through the use of library-centered, independent study with a bibliographically expert faculty.

One of the ten other institutions that described its experimenting at Wakulla Springs was Antioch College in Yellow Springs, Ohio. My own earliest interest in the Library-College idea came from that campus during a visit in 1928. There I experienced what they had then just originated—the autonomous course, in which the student studied independently under bibliographic advice by the faculty. It was reassuring to hear Dr. Sam Baskin 35 years later describing the Antioch learning mode as basically independent study, in the autonomous course tradition, reinforced by the work-study idea that had been introduced by Arthur Morgan there nearly four decades before.

Under Dr. Baskin's leadership the Union for Research and Experimentation was organized. It is an association of ten colleges—Antioch, Bard, Goddard, Hofstra, Illinois Teachers College—North, Monteith, Nasson, Sarah Lawrence, Shimer, and Stephens, that have joined to encourage innovation in undergraduate education. Aided by a U.S.O.E. grant, the Union spearheaded a conference on innovation at Magnolia, Mass., in May 1966. About 40 colleges were represented by presidents, deans, professors, and students, and some dozen philanthropic government and professional agencies as well as manufacturers of computers and other educational equipment participated.

Proceedings of the Magnolia Conference will reveal a heavy innovational accent, by the experimenting colleges represented, on the independent study mode. For example, Dean Stafford North of

Oklahoma Christian College described his carrel-centered independent study program in which every student has his own individual workbench in the Library Learning Resource Center, with dial access to a variety of media formats. The Library-College idea was described by President Dan Sillers of Jamestown, and a committee, subsequently, amplified and refined the Jamestown charter.

Finally, in December of that year, the Drexel conference on the Library College was held at the Bellevue-Stratford Hotel in Philadelphia. An amazing number—some 200—college presidents, professors, librarians, and agency representatives registered. The keynote address by Chancellor Harvie Branscomb, Emeritus of Vanderbilt University, author of the classic Carnegie Corporation sponsored study *Teaching with Books* challenged classroom and library faculty, together, to refine the independent study learning mode, adapt it to serve, not only the gifted, but the whole range of abilities, now found in our expanded collece student population.

These four innovational conferences—Wakulla Springs, Jamestown, Magnolia, and Philadelphia—have been cited as representative of the growing higher educational compulsion to experiment. To quote from "Project Changeover" of the Union for Research and Experimentation:

> "Students, faculty, college administrators, and critics from off the campus have long expressed need for major improvements in college teaching. Several factors now make rapid advance imperative."

The factors the Union cited are five, all pertinent to Elmira's changeover:

1. "Increased size of the student population creating a need for new programs to maintain quality instruction while serving many more students.

2. "a greater variety of students requiring different approaches in both content and methodology

3. "accelerated social change suggesting students must be prepared to live in a world that will differ markedly from the one in which their parents and teachers grew up

4. "explosion of knowledge brings pressure to change the content of instruction

5. "new technology is producing unprecedented possibilities for

the development of a new 'mix' of resources for teaching and learning."

Well, here we are, with the compulsions to change. What do you change, and how, and why? I need not tell you how ready our age is to expose what's wrong with anything, from Viet Nam abroad, to minorities at home. No one is really interested in what is right with us, and it would be a miracle if any conviction on a solution to a major problem ever occurred.

Let me begin then by declaring that college faculties all over these United States have done a tremendously fine job of higher education. And I mean it, when I say I am deeply impressed by what you have done at Elmira. Because of my editorial experience, college catalogs have been a part of my regular reading. I consider your 1967-68 format one of the most distinctive and creative among my collection of 2,000 college catalogs. More absorbing than even the format, is the content. You can understand how aroused I was by finding at the very beginning the words

"The Elmira curriculum emphasizes independent study . . ." which means you and I agree with Winslow Hatch when he observes that one measure of quality higher education is the degree to which students can and do study independently.

I now propose to consider with you some of the ways and means. Let me refer to the Library-College Charter once more:

"The charter assumes that the 'Library-College' concept can and should be adapted to colleges with varying objectives and philosophies. The curriculum of a particular Library-College must emerge from its objectives and philosophy." In order, I share with you some thoughts on four elements in the Library-College: 1) Something I call *The Learning Mode*; 2) *Curriculum*; 3) *Learning Resources*; 4) Our Changing *Faculty Role*.

THE LEARNING MODE

Before someone else, let me say first, the students come first. How many times at teachers' conventions have I witnessed the torpedoing of an innovative proposal with a stultiloquy, much like the dinner table when right at your punch line someone says "Pass the cream." There can be no doubt that all of us who gladly or even sadly teach aim to put the students above all other considerations. Our only differences are on how best to do this.

Right off I may invite your dissent. I believe learning is a struggle. There is no slick road to culture. Somewhere in the process we have to struggle and suffer alone. This is not to say medicine has to be bitter to be good. It is to say that passive learning is inadequate. And one of my basic quarrels with the classroom mode is that it tends to encourage more activity in the teacher than in the student. In these forty years of teaching, going back to my brief and ineffectual efforts with infants in the third grade, and with early adolescents in the east side New York junior high school, as well as in the over three decades in both undergraduate and graduate campus classrooms, I checked myself asking "how am *I* doing" rather than how are *they* doing.

Because of this, I found myself steadily moving toward bibliographic advising, but not as too many librarians do it. Rather it began with bubbling over a book, or a periodical article, or a federal document I accidentally discovered when looking for something else, or just even aimlessly browsing because I am eerily drawn to the mysterious silence of library stacks and a strange fragrance of buckram. Here was the true meaning of serendipity, a word science fiction introduced to the sciences too long after the other culture had learned it from an 18th century novelist. And so my students became princes and princesses of serendipity and began reporting their findings with that blaze in their eyes that we all have treasured in our teaching days.

But serendipity was only one part of the independent study idea. Years ago I had accidently discovered in high school another element in the library learning mode. In my senior year I elected a course in economics, offered for the first time, because it sounded like a college subject. But along with the other boys I had another reason. The teacher was young and very pretty, and I experienced one of my earliest and most painful "crushes." I wanted so very much to do well in that class.

So I went to the high school library and read the general article on economics in the Britannica. It gave me an overview of the subject. The result was that I anticipated each unit of the subject in that class as it was introduced by that very beautiful lady teacher. When she followed the Britannica's sequence and content I nodded my head triumphantly; when she did not I quarreled with her silently or sometimes even openly. I earned my A in that class largely because of that encyclopedia overview. Throughout my college days thereafter, I always preceded each term with overview encyclopedia readings of all the subjects represented by the courses in which I planned to enroll. To some extent this early accidental discovery of the power of the encyclopedia overview in learning influenced me to devote so much of my life to the study, evaluation, designing and editing of encyclopedias.

The foundation of independent study is reading. Perhaps my Fulbright year in the United Kingdom, plus my observations in universities on the continent strengthened this concept. In England, as you know, students and faculty do not speak of enrolling in a course in Economics, or Philosophy, or even Mathematics, as much as they speak of Reading in Economics, or Reading in Philosophy, or even Reading in Mathematics. I do not deny that reading is a struggle, much more with some writing than with other, frequently because of the nature of the content, and sometimes because of the inarticulateness of the author, but that very struggle is antagonistic to passivity and may even drive the student to conference, seminar, or classroom lecture.

Another characteristic of the Library-College learning mode is a reversal of the classroom-library sequence. It may mean, as a start, following the Oklahoma Christian concept as explained by Stafford North. A three-semester hour course, enrolled in by a student constitutes a contract with the professor to devote 9 clock hours a week to that subject. But this contract does not necessarily mean what it does in class contact institutions, namely three class meetings a week and six hours of outside preparation, on the formula of one for two. Rather the weekly calendar may be so flexible, at the teacher and student's option, that some weeks might have nine scheduled hours in the student's private carrel in the library and no class meeting at all; or eight scheduled carrel reading periods and one class period as unscheduled as library reading for students usually is now.

At this point, let it be made clear that reading can be done in other formats than hard cover print, or paperback, or periodical, or any other medium produced by a press. "Reading" writes *Saturday Review's* Frank Jennings, "remember is not restricted to the printed page. Actually it never was. In one reading is the art of transmitting the ideas, facts and feelings from the mind and soul of an author to the mind and soul of a reader . . . throughout his history man has 'read' many things: the flight of birds, the guts of sheep, sun spots, liver spots and the life lines on a hand. He has read the lore of the jungle, the spoor of the beast, and the portents in a dish of tea." Reading in the Library-College means communication between the student and his teacher through any and every medium, sensory and extra-sensory, that exists. In the Library-College the book is basic, but the book is what I have called the Generic Book.

The learning mode of the Library-College, therefore, is basically what you have indicated in the Elmira Catalog, "Independent Study" under faculty bibliographic advice in the generic book. But the Learning Mode includes also something we call performance. This consists of writing and speaking; acting, singing, dancing. It might include painting, sculpture, ceramics and the other visual arts. Nor are the recreational arts excluded, athletics of all kinds—tennis, swimming, self-defense. A very special area of performance is in the practical arts, including the skills of home making, driver competence, cosmetology, and of course, health education.

A final aspect of the Library-College learning mode is the adaptation of Dr. Frank Laubach's "Each One Teach One" principle. Whether Joseph Lancaster or Andrew Bell was the real originator of the monitorial system of instruction under which older students tutored younger ones in fundamentals, the fact remains there is a mutual advantage in this method especially for independent study. Most of us will attest that we reinforced what we learned in college the first year we had to teach it. This would be the advantage to the sophomore who undertook to review with a Freshman. And for the freshman, the more frequent conferences with the sophomore would interleave seminar and conference with faculty. If Each One Teach One were initiated with junior-sophomore and senior-junior teams as well, an immediate role in the Elmira change over would be provided for the upper classmen as well as for the freshmen. For example, the problem of transition in any innovation has often proved a deterrent. By drawing from the old, upper classmen could contribute to the new curriculum. Besides the Each One Teach One, offers and on-campus opportunity for the Work-Study motive exist.

CURRICULUM CHANGEOVER

When the General Education movement of the post World War II years with some struggle induced Chemistry, Physics, and Geology professors to offer an integrated Physical Science course for freshmen, an important step toward Gestalt was taken. It wasn't easy on our campus. I served year after year on a University General Education committee, the only dean invited to serve by the faculty. It was so difficult to get the physicist to think of his course as anything but physics, with a few imposed peripheries. And each September we would be confronted all over again by specialists' backslidings with cumulated evidence that students were confused by the mishmash. But those of us who believed the students deserved a departmentalized synthesis of knowledge persisted, and Bi Sci replaced separated botany, physiology, and zoology; Social Science superseded separated sociology, political science, economics; and a Humanities course that related philosophy, religion, literature, music and the visual arts to each other triumphed.

The next step has been a long time coming. I see it in Elmira's new interdisciplinary Liberal Studies course. At this writing, there were only the statements in the Bulletin and in the pink and processed announcements. What I propose may therefore be fully covered. Nevertheless I plead for consideration of two neglected or underestimated curriculum areas.

The first of these I call "Media" for want of a better descriptive title. Perhaps the nearest thing to it that we have had in the past have been the perfunctory library tours during freshmen orientation week. On some campuses we have also units on library use in the freshman English classes, or even a whole one semester course, elective or required, on the library. At its best such instruction has fallen far short, certainly, for what a changeover to independent study requires. One of my longest quarrels with teacher education has been the incidental treatment of instructional materials. Only comparatively recently have state certifications begun to require for elementary teachers especially as much as a separate three-semester hour course on learning resources. Such a course should comprehend the three separate offers frequently found on our campuses, in Children's Literature, Library Use, Audio Visual Education. To accomplish this, I wrote the book *Instructional Materials*, as a sort of marriage license for what has frequently been referred to as the "shotgun marriage" in Florida of librarians and audiovisualists.

What I propose is that as part of Basic Liberal studies, students be given a course in media *per se*, not incidentally, as we have never yet accomplished. Such a mastery should enable our students to move among the resources more confidently than our generation is able to do even today. For example, on the open shelves of every college library so-called Reference Room is a collection of information retrievers such as even our Information Scientists haven't fully explored. The other day a colleague of mine and close friend who is a professor of physics was sitting in my office chatting when I was interrupted by an urgent long distance call. When I finished, I found my colleague engrossed by the newest issue of the *Statesman's Yearbook,* which was on my table for review.

Because I know him real well he said to me unashamedly, "Where has this book been all of my professional life? Has it been published long?" "Gunter," I said apologetically, "this is a 104th annual issue. It's one of our Reference classics and a particular favorite of mine. I'm glad that you a physicist find it related to your interests." His enthusiasm for its contents was unbounded, and his embarrassment at his ignorance of its existence painful. "My fault, Gunter," I said, and I meant it. Reference books are my specialty. As an English teacher I consider the literature of reference as exciting as almost any other one of the literary forms I have studied and taught. Yet I have somehow failed to communicate their potential to so many of the generation I have taught and been associated with.

Except for encyclopedias and dictionaries, and possibly atlases, I am not sure that most of our students are even aware that as many as 15,000 or more different reference titles exist in the world, and that even among the one to 10% of that number on college library shelves can be found the means to cope with what we tritely call the information explosion. Certainly if the half of knowledge is knowing where to find it, do we not owe our students a thorough training in the scope and arrangement of the basic reference books? And not only reference books, but other media of all formats, levels and subjects, as well as modern library organization with its increasing attention to automation and hardware.

The second of these units I have called in my Library-College curriculum, simply Knowledge. In library classifications like Dewey Decimal or Library of Congress, we have a class sometimes called "generalia" where books that cover all of knowledge as a unity, like encyclopedias, are classified. This describes the course or the unit I should like to see in our curricula twice, once at the beginning as a preface to separated specialism, and once at the end of the four years as a sort of capstone synthesis.

Without detailing the content let me broadly sketch two major components. One part acknowledges the debt to the older generation by overviewing the knowledge considered of greatest significance to scholars. Indeed in my designing and editing of encyclopedias, I have always gone along with the definition "a summary of the knowledge most significant to mankind." This would define my concept of the first component, and indeed a good encyclopedia studied judiciously might well be a textbook for this component.

The other component salutes the younger generation. I would approach this part of the Knowledge course by designing with each student for herself what we call in Information Science, an Interest Profile. I would ask each student to list frankly her most significant current interests, in order from one to ten, encourage her to differ with the significances of the older generation. Indeed, if she were at all aware of the intellectual blue blood approach to higher education, the kind that Chicago and Robert Hutchins flaunted in earlier decades, I would encourage her to dissent. I would encourage her to put at the top of her list her keenest interest regardless of how unintelligent it might be. The students' interest profile would constitute an important half of this Knowledge course.

One of the first independent studies would be a literature search for sources of information about the interests of greatest significance, not only to the older generation of scholars, but to the younger generation of students. In this search students would have the advice of the faculty. A composite of Student Interest Profiles would be currently maintained in the library. A faculty-librarian follow-up on these profiles would be what Information Science calls SDI (Selective Dissemination of Information). Both current and retrospective library accessions are continuously searched against these Interest Profiles and references of individual interest communicated to the students concerned.

This communication is more than a bibliographic notice. It is a professional prescription by a faculty adviser who sensitively matches individual differences in students with individual differences in media, by subject, level, format. Here is a student who had trouble with a botany process as described in printed words who suddenly understands by means clear to her by a time-lapse 16 mm motion picture. Here is another student whose appreciation of Hamlet's soliloqy is enhanced by concurrent listening to John Gielgud.

Perhaps these two examples provide a modulation from curriculum to Library Learning Resources.

LIBRARY LEARNING RESOURCES

After the site is selected, architect and librarian settle down to planning three major accommodations: for the students, for stock, for staff. Formerly our standards required that 25% of the student body should be seated in the library. That standard has steadily upped with the trend to independent study. As you know, Oklahoma Christian designed its library resources center to accommodate in individual carrels 110% of its student body. I recommend this for Elmira, to take care of student population growth.

Next, the carrel is destined to replace not only the conventional library reading table, but the classroom arm chair as well. Mount San Antonio originally designed reader accommodation in its new library building 50% conventional reading room tables; 50% carrels. After less than a year's operation they converted half of their tables to carrels. (The Ford Foundation booklet containing 16 different carrel designs also illustrates how to convert a conventional reading table.)

Since the name of your new building suggests considerable provision for hardware and the so-called newer media, you will probably want to provide at the outset for so-called wet carrels, with dial access to a variety of media formats. The wet carrel will reinforce audio-tutorial laboratory such as Purdue pioneered.

Stock accommodation now goes beyond the basic stack planning for print of all kinds. It includes housing and maintenance for graphics, projections like films, filmstrips, transparencies; for tapes and discs; for slides, microprojections and micro formats; for programmed materials; and for the components and hardware that accompany these media. Electronic, automated, and computerized innovations become more startling daily. About some of these, like the printout catalog, I am excited; about others I advise restraint.

Staff accommodation heretofore limited to about 100 square feet per full time employee in library organization is now being augmented some to provide office space for all or nearly all of the faculty. Recently I have consulted on new library resource centers where such faculty accommodation is being favored over scattering faculty offices in other buildings on the campus. Certainly the independent study trend favors such faculty accommodation in the library learning resource center.

For Dallas Baptist College I have suggested in cooperation with a creative and innovative architect that a square building be designed, a most economical construction. The center square accommodates stock, returning to the traditional fixed stack on tiers that are a standard 7′ 6″ high. The square that surrounds the center accommodates students in carrels, varied in design so as not to give quite the Alcatraz appearance that occurs when carrels are blocked together. This square has the same heights as the stacks; but the outer square which accommodates faculty offices, seminars, a classroom, lecture hall as well as other staff space is about 11 feet high, resulting in three stack-carrel levels for every two room levels.

CHANGING FACULTY ROLE

Change inevitably introduces some insecurity in all of us. Since I am of the older faculty generation, I confess to more than average amount of resistance. I am troubled about our contemporary rejection of values that still include for me some of the elements of that eternal verity we seek in the ultimate. Because of that very quest for perfection which our profession seems to imply, we as teachers, more than any other occupation in the world, cannot oppose change that promises improvement.

Critically we must admit that classroom-centered teaching is less suited to coping with the ever widening range of individual differences created by universal higher education. Nor can word-of-mouth communication, necessary when other media—print, audiovisual, environmental—were few and limited in variety. Today, probably for the first time in the history of education we can match individual differences in students with individual differences in media. And this matching of media to individual students so that we will light a fire in them is the essence of our new role.

So to begin with we must not only increase our awareness of our students individually, but we must gain a new insight into the universe of media. We must know them not only by subject, but by level, and by format. Only through such knowledge can we match individual differences in students with individual differences in materials. In our new role we become much like the good physician, prescribing for the mental health and intellectual, esthetic and spiritual improvement of our students much as the family physician used to prescribe for his patients. Advisement thus takes on a new dimension, a most rewarding one as we watch new worlds open for our students, frequently through serendipity. Our role now includes greater responsibility for media selection. We read, review, preview, pre-aud now with the individual student profiles before us constantly. We encourage increasing independence in our students at their workbench carrels. Selectively we disseminate information to them through suggested media, through their upper classmen tutors, in individual conferences, in seminar discussions with groups, through lectures covering our specialties and enthusiasms with content and format available in any other media.

We evaluate with a new challenge. There is a certain dualism created by the changeover. We must prove to ourselves, to our students and to measuring agencies that what we are doing is better than what is being done conventionally. Therefore we must measure first of all with traditional instruments—standardized tests. But we must also devise new measures that reveal what is going on inside of our students, intellectually, emotionally, spiritually as well as skillfully.

EPILOGUE

Recently I have begun to reread the 150 letters from our alumni handsomely bound for me as one of my retirement gifts. In my former students' touching words are greater rewards than are offered any other occupation in our society. As I look back at my long and good life with colleagues and students, I am certain I would make the same decision again. Part of my reason is this constant urge to transmit to the next generation the best that man has done and been.

I sincerely believe the changeover from classroom teaching to carrel learning is a worthwhile innovation. It provides a better opportunity to match individual differences in our students. It copes more effectively with the information acceleration. And I believe it offers us as faculty the most creative teaching opportunity we have yet known. Along the Library-College Way, I congratulate you, my colleagues, in innovation for your bold and promising changeover. May you all experience the satisfaction I have known.

3.

THE COLLEGE BECOMES A LIBRARY

(Essay for the Library-College conference, Drexel Institute of Technology, Philadelphia, December, 1966.)

THE COLLEGE of the immediate future will be a library. All the trends of the present point to independent study by the student as the dominant pattern of American higher education. Group teaching in a classroom is relentlessly being subordinated to individual learning in a carrel. The faculty is lecturing information less, and guiding bibliographically more. And that part of the faculty called "professional librarian" is more willing than ever to let clericals and automation take over management and housekeeping chores so that at long last librarianship may devote itself to one of its high roles—education. What is emerging, inevitably, from the trend to independent study is what we call the Library-College.

Others may offer better variations on this definition. To me a Library-College is a college in which the dominant learning mode is independent study by the student in the Library, bibliographically guided, intellectually aroused, and spiritually stirred by the faculty.

The *learning mode* of the Library-College is universal, and followed by all students regardless of their individual differences.

The *library* of the Library-College is selected to match the individual differences in the student population of the college community. All subjects, levels, and formats are represented in the collection. In this library the term book means the "generic book," which comprises all the media through which educator and educand communicate.

The *faculty* of the Library-College is a cross between today's teaching-committed librarian and library-using teacher.

The *curriculum* of the Library-College is the sum total of the students' experience under the influence of the college. Content is interdisciplinary, crossing the sacred boundary lines of predatory disciplines, and exposing to the student interstices often excluded from consideration in the current college courses of study. Specialisms are cushioned by general education in the beginning that integrates not alone within the sciences, the social sciences, and the humanities; but *among* them; and at the end by a capstone synthesis.

The *facility* of the Library-College is fundamentally a library learning resource center, surrounded by laboratories, gymnasium-athletic fields, auditoria, residences, recreational, health, and meditation and worship areas.

The *organization* of the Library-College is committed to encouraging intimate informality in learning. Its total student body numbers under 500. As enrollments increase, new colleges are opened, and gathered into a cluster, Cambridge University-like.

From this overview some specifications for the Library-College are offered both confidently and diffidently.

EVOLUTION OF THE LIBRARY-COLLEGE IDEA

The Library-College was inevitable once printing was invented and books became ever more plentiful. What hastened this inevitability was the concurrent spread of educational opportunity to everyone, first on the elementary, then on the secondary, and now even on the higher educational level. Because of the ever widening range of individual differences, group teaching in the classroom became steadily less communicative to more students. With the proliferation of print and other media, independent learning in the library became insistently more rewarding.

In 1880, Justin Winsor, eminent historian and the first president of the American Library Association, who was then directing Harvard's Library toward newer educational opportunities, wrote, in his eight-page contribution for the U.S. Bureau's historic document,

> "I will not say that the library is the antagonist of the textbook; but it is, I claim, its generous rival and abettor,

> helping where it fails and leading where it falters. If this is so, it follows that *we must build our libraries with classrooms annexed,* and we must learn our way through the wilderness of books until we have the instinct of the red man when he knows the north by the thickness of the treboles. . .
>
> The proposition then is to make the library the grand rendezvous of the college for teacher and pupil alike, and to do it in as much of the teaching as is convenient and practicable."[1]

Perhaps Justin Winsor's essay was one of the earliest implementations of the Carlyle philosophy and the herald of the independent study movement. Just which U.S. college was the birthplace of the so-called honors program is less important than the fact that through numerous variations at Harvard, Princeton, Swarthmore, Colgate, Antioch, Southwestern in Memphis, Stephens, Oberlin, Rollins and a score or more campuses the learning accent was shifting from classroom to library.

The movement began to gain impetus after World War I. Typically, Swarthmore's Honors Program was described in 1927:

> "Topics are assigned by professors a fortnight or more in advance, with brief indication of the literature available. Such bibliographical suggestions are never complete and it is always understood that the student must ransack the library for additional sources."[2]

At Colgate, a few years later, President Cutten defined the aim of their "preceptorial" variation on the independent study theme "as that of broadening the intellectual horizon. . . developing the student intellectually as a whole man. . . In general we find this aim is best achieved by stimulating the leading interest of the college man along lines which might not occur to him. For this purpose we have extensive reading lists and reading facilities . . . The reading, however, is not compulsory for the group, the whole thing being at the discretion of the faculty member in question."[3]

Sample descriptions of innovations in learning mode that featured varieties of independent study can be extracted from the pre-World War II higher educational literature. Notable examples would include Lamar Johnson's "Vitalized Library" at Stephens;[4] President Conant's "Hobby Study"[5] at Harvard; President Diehl's Tutorial Plan at Southwestern, Memphis; President Arthur Morgan's Autonomous Courses at Antioch. Possibly the impact of a September visit in 1928 to an Antioch beginning Economics class crystallized a cumulative urge for independent library study in my own undergraduate days.

It was the opening day. As I recall it, the professor gave the students a syllabus; a list of basic sources in Economics; his office hours and room number; and a calendar of quiz, essay, mid-term, and final examination dates. As I remember, there were only four lectures scheduled for the whole semester, on subjects not covered by print, and upon which the professor was an expert. One of these lectures was the one I heard on the opening class day: an inspired overview of the subject of Economics, such as might rarely occur in one of the better general encyclopedias. At the conclusion of the lecture, the Professor distributed a list of possible subjects for investigation, and the form in which the investigations were to be reported. Only the first topic was required of every one and was due in two weeks. Three other subjects were to be selected by the student from the list, or independently in conference with the professor. His final words to the class, "Happy library hunting; the next time we meet as a class will be at the first of the term's four scheduled lectures, unless you request a class meeting before."

POST WORLD WAR II DEVELOPMENTS

Up through V-J Day the independent study movement was a phenomenon reserved for the superior student—"the upper 10%" who had inherited the intellectual talents labelled educationally as "gifted." But in the two decades that followed, this nation boldly committed itself to a "first" in the history of the world: not only to educate, but to higher educate every one. There is no time here to endorse this commitment, philosophically and enthusiastically, except, telescopically. Fundamentally I believe all of us are gifted in some directions; less talented in others. This goes for the so-called "10%" as well as for the other "90%." Historically, I observe that violent revolutions (political) have occurred when the 10% and the 90% were educationally so far removed from each other that they were no longer able to communicate. The hope here is that universal higher education will lay a foundation for gradual rather than explosive political and social change.

Whether these philosophical assumptions can be defended or not the fact remains that universal higher education in the United States is almost here in 1966. With the help of the exciting junior college phenomenon it has become almost anti-social for the high school graduate to go anywhere except to college. By 1970, we are told, there will be a million students in college, the highest per cent ever of that age group.

What confronts those of us who gladly or sadly teach are two phenomena unknown to higher education before, at least in such proportions. One of these is the growing threat of impersonality caused by numbers. Mob scenes in gymnasia on registration days have become a major obstacle to higher education in our so-called multiversities. The other hazard is in the classroom, group teaching of the widest range of individual differences among students ever before enrolled in our colleges. Unless students can be communicated with more individually than numbers, and talent diversifications permit in the classroom, the present spasmodic, student insurrections will grow into a continuous rebellion.

Fortunately, solutions for both problems are at hand. The hazard of numbers can be met by reorganization of our multiversities into cluster colleges. For the first time in the history of education it is now possible to meet individual differences in students with individual differences in media.

Parallelling the college student population growth, which our pedagogical orators like to call one of the several "explosions," media of all formats have been proliferating in geometric proportions. The beginning may have occurred in Mainz, Germany, about 1450, if the invention of printing is credited to Johannes Guttenberg Gensfleisch. As the making of books increased, and various new formats entered the educational world, the quantity and range of subjects and levels prolificated as well. By the beginning of the 19th century, no library apologized for the presence of non-manuscript material as did the Duke of Urbino in the 15th century when he noted:

> "In this library all the books are superlatively good, and written with pen, and had there been one printed volume it would have been ashamed in such company."[6]

Rather, libraries began to accession other forms of print: newspapers, periodicals, pamphlets, broadsides, minibooks. The introduction of photography brought pictures into the collection. How early other graphics entered the library is indefinite, but bulletin boards and exhibits steadily became important library media of communication. Nor is the inclusion of museum objects a very recent library phenomenon. Certainly maps and globes have had a centuries-old place in libraries.

Toward the end of the last century, probably in the St. Louis school system, Superintendent W. T. Harris, later to become U. S. Commissioner of Education, added the graphic, realia, and geographic media to the newly invented phonorecording and motion picture to herald what was later to become known as the audiovisual movement. Although some librarians persisted in referring to these newer formats, and to radio, TV, teaching machines and computer consoles as "non-book," much in the manner of the Duke of Urbino on print in the 15th century, there was no question that all of these newer media were part of the "generic book."

The proliferation of media since World War II armed librarianship to lead the educational world to meet the challenge of universal education. Ever since Binet and Cattell at the turn of this century, pedagogy had been paying lip service to something called "individual differences" without really doing very much about it. Pedagogy could not, as long as it was tied to the lockstep of classroom group teaching. Nor was Pedagogy likely to have much help from a librarianship that, on the school and college level, made a fetish of supporting classroom instruction. In the words of Harvie Banscomb in that monumental volume *Teaching with Books*:

> "To sum up, it may be said without hesitation that the fundamental need of the college library is to develop a distinctive program of its own. Absorbed as it has been in the task of increasing its supply of books and compelled to serve a constantly increasing student body, paying small salaries and getting usually-although not always—no more than it paid for, it has been too imitative of the other institutions."[7]

Well, the proliferation of media provides Librarianship with the opportunity to develop a distinctive program of its own.

In 1934 at the Chicago Century of Progress A.L.A. convention I read my paper on the "Library-Arts College." It was described as "the logical culmination of such current trends in American higher education as are exemplified by honors courses, comprehensive examinations and other reforms . . ." and differing from the conventional college in at least five essentials: 1) a learning mode that reverses the library-classroom relationship by having the latter support; 2) an educational plant that consists of a library, which contains all of the classrooms and laboratories as well as the reading facilities; 3) an instructional method that borrows the "each one teach one" principle of the Bell-Lancaster monitorial schools; 4) a faculty that is bibliographically competent to guide student independent study in the library, and generalist enough to cross sacred disciplines' boundary lines; 5) a curriculum which follows the library, rather than *vice versa,* which school and college libraries proclaim so self-righteously, now.

Well here was a distinctive program of its own for the American college library. Few will remember the shock and indignation with which this proposal was met some three decades ago. As Dr. Branscomb might have observed, librarians, more than educators, considered the proposal preposterous. I recall that in my youthful feeling of discouragement I compared my Chicago reception with the booing Stravinsky got in Paris about a quarter of a century before, for introducing a new musical dimension.

All during those dark, Hitler pre-war days I studied innovation in our U.S. colleges for features that might reenforce the library-arts college idea. I took notes constantly, sketched a campus plan, and sought to enlist financial backing for a prototype college. But these were post-depression WPA years, and my meager college librarian's salary prohibited even minor expenditures for explorations. Pearl Harbor relegated the stack of notes to a farm house in Michigan as I went off to war. But I never forgot the idea. Even in the far off China-Burma-India theatre (my war-time substitute for my library CBI) I used to discuss the Library-Arts College with an intelligent staff sergeant, whose father was fairly affluent, and who promised that if he came out alive he would work with me to establish the college. But he was killed in action.

Nevertheless, upon discharge from the army in the spring of 1946, a friend and I set out to establish a Library-Arts College in South Florida. We almost succeeded in Sarasota. With the help of a newspaperman there and several prominent citizens we nearly enlisted the Crosley family to donate their estate, close by the present airport, as a site, and as the first building. But as the last moment, the Crosleys decided to sell instead, and after following up a few more futile leads in Venice and Miami, we accepted President Campbell's invitation to join the Florida State University faculty.

I had just decided that if the Library-Arts College was ever to be tried out anywhere I would have to write another book, when Bob Jordan sent me an announcement of the Kenyon Talkshop. Since 1962 I have lived Library-College as I never have before, because of Bob Jordan, Lamar Johnson, Dan Sillers, Pat Knapp, Lee Sutton, Dan Bergen, John Harvey and all of the others you will find in the *Library-College* volume. In that year, two fellow deans and I on our way to join a Southern Association evaluation team for Texas Tech at Lubbock began talking experimental college at Florida State University. Two other deans, the Director of the University Library and the chairman of our department of Higher Education joined us, and one night a week, for a full year, we met in one of our homes to design our prototype college for the eventual cluster organization of the university. Of course, the Library-College concept received regular and full attention. At these meetings, we planned also the Wakulla Springs Colloquium at which ten invited experimenting institutions from California, Michigan, Ohio, Iowa, Missouri and Florida described their innovations.[9]

Innovation is of urgent concern to higher education today. The Magnolia, Massachusetts conference of May 1966 revealed the commitments of additional colleges. Perhaps no description there of an experiment in operations seemed farther along the way toward a Library-College than that by Stafford North of Oklahoma Christian. Elsewhere, unmistakable features of the Library-College can be found at Antioch, where the autonomus course approach has now been extended to the entire freshman class; at Florida Presbyterian, where classes are replaced completely by independent study in the library during the winter inter-term; at Parsons, Monteith, Okland Community College, where components of the concept are being successfully demonstrated; and of course, at Jamestown, the first college to commit itself to the idea.

THE COLLEGE BECOMES A LIBRARY

THE LIBRARY-COLLEGE

Permit me now to sketch my designs for six elements of the Library-College. They are only sketches and certainly open to suggestion. In order, I wish to consider with you: 1) Learning Mode; 2) Library; 3) Faculty; 4) Curriculum; 5) Facility; 6) Organization.

Of the Learning Mode enough has been said to emphasize the locus shift from group teaching in the classroom to individual learning in the carrel. The philosophy of this mode was well put for Bennington College when education was conceived as "intellectual adventure rather than indoctrination,"[10] and the college bulletin announced as a principal aim "to accustom its students to the habit of engaging voluntarily in learning rather than submitting involuntarily at certain periods to formal instruction."[11]

In the Library-College the student is learning primarily by reading. This is not unlike the English university where the student records not that he is attending a class in economics but rather that he is reading in Economics, or in Physics, or in Philosophy, or Greek, or whatever. Although a major part of this reading is done in the format known as the hard cover, the Library-College faculty guides and encourages students to read in all formats. Such reading may include listening to tapes and discs, viewing transparencies, filmstrips, motion pictures; listening and viewing radio, television, and the entire repertoire of educational media formats; it may, indeed, enlist sensory experiencing with all of the five senses. To quote *Saturday Review's* Frank G. Jennings:

> "But reading, remember, is not restricted to the printed page. Actually it never was . . . throughout his history man has 'read' many things: the flight of birds, the guts of sheep, sun spots, liver spots, and the life lines on a hand. He has read the lore of the jungle, the spoor of the beast and the portents in a dish of tea. But whatever he has read and however he has read, it has always been for 'reason'."[12]

Yes, reading encompasses the generic book in all of its formats. In the course of his college life student reading will add up to all of the sensory responses to his environment. And learning will come through that mystical extrasensory flash which we are only beginning to investigate in some of the "far out" parapsychological laboratories like the ones at Duke. To encourage this extrasensory perception on the part of the student, reading should include also meditation, and deep introspection on such impractical questions as "Who am I?" "Where did I come from?" "Why am I here?"

But in the Library-College the student is also learning by doing, by demonstrating, by performing, by manipulating, and by speaking, writing and teaching. One measure of an educated man or woman is the ability to communicate. In the Library-College the student will write as well as read. He will write well and frequently—reports, papers, essays, and even imaginative literature, including poetry. He will speak informally in conferences with faculty and fellow students, with continuous, conscious and critical effort to improve the form of his speech and add a creative element to it.

The Library-College student will strive to do the many things required to maintain life. Part of each day will be devoted to perfecting himself in the tasks of homemaking and earning a living. This may involve agriculture and horticulture on the college farms; carpentering in the shops; cooking, sewing, home maintenance and repair; auto driving and servicing. He will practice the art of self-defense under expert instruction; learn to swim, and perfect himself in a sport of his own choice. And there will be both intramural and intercollegiate athletics. Yes, even football, and the team will be coached and urged on to win, to strive for the coveted number one in the AP weekly poll, and to aim to take on the winner of the pro super bowl, to prove that college football is better than the professional brand, even as certain students of the game like the late General Neyland of Tennessee, and Earl Blake of the Army, and most recently in *Sports Illustrated,* John Sutherland. Because I believe football has a unique place in education and in our national life. And it has far more color, and meaning than is revealed in Ernest Hemingway's glorification of the bull fight.

The Library-College student will perform in any of the arts he selects: music, the dance, sculpture, painting, architecture. The college theatre will offer opportunity for every dramatic talent. Editing and writing experience beyond that afforded by educational assignments will be available through college publications, all joint faculty-student ventures, from campus newspaper through annual, and monthly literary and humor magazines. If campus or community radio and television stations exist these will be added performance opportunities.

Not the least performing opportunity will be the "each one-teach one" requirement of all students. Toward the end of the 18th century two English educators, Andrew Bell (1753-1832) and Joseph Lancaster (1778-1838) each claimed to have originated the "monitorial" system of instruction under which advanced students drilled their juniors in fundamentals. In recent years this system has been used by the missionary Dr. Lubach to advance literacy in backward nations. The advantage of this system is mutual to both monitor and learner. Every one who has ever taught will affirm that knowledge is reenforced by the teaching of it. The monitorial system is especially made to order for an independent study program.

There are other characteristics of the Library-College Learning Mode. One dramatic device to stimulate fact learning is to adapt the GE television "College Bowl" for intramural competitions. The questions can be selected from various national examinations which students may need to take at times and whose outcomes may reflect on the college. Public debates, addresses, forums, panels are other devices. Above all else the Learning Mode aims to be student initiated, individual, and independent.

THE LIBRARY

The Library-College Library is, to paraphrase Carlyle, the true college, since it is primarily a collection of books. But the book in the Library-College Library is the generic book. It includes a selection of every subject, level, and format pertinent to the educational mission. Subject selection reflects not only the curriculum disciplines we accept today, but some areas that fall outside and in between. An example might be the subjects beyond the borderlines of science, the occult, flying saucers, and Bridie Murphy. Levels should represent the range of individual differences in the student population of a particular college community. This could mean school encyclopedia level of science for some; post graduate for others.

When it comes to format, my classification of the Generic Book as it appears in my book *Instructional Materials* is a beginning.[14] There are at least a hundred or more physical makeups of educational media found in the schools and colleges of the nation. Representations of all or most of them belong in the collection if only because one kind of format will communicate better with the background of an individual student for a particular learning situation. It is fashionable, intellectually, these days to quote Marshall McLuhan on media. I have served with him on the ASCD Instructional Materials Commission. Much of what he says does not communicate with me. But this much I have believed all of these years of my educational effort to effect a marriage between audio-visualists and librarians: "the form of the medium may influence communication." Indeed it is entirely possible that format may change meaning for different individuals. If this is so, then it is more important than ever that the Library stock representative items in all formats. Nor should so-called audio-visual media ever be considered non-book material, and therefore reduced in its educational status.

Furthermore, new dimensions of access to these materials must now be envisaged. The open stack is certainly made to order for the Library-College. But so also is the recent extension of remote access. If the carrel is to become truly the student's work bench, the Library-College Library must be prepared to go as far as possible from dry through damp to wet carrel. For our glossary, I understand the wet carrel to mean carrel equipped with dial access to audio and visual material like tape, disc, radio; to still projections like transparencies, slides, film strips, and possibly to closed circuit television, and remote console, computer-assisted instruction; to facsimile and radioteletype, etc. "Dampness" to me represents various stages along the way from dry to wet carrels.

With regard to bibliographic access, we should look forward to the computerized printout book catalog as an eventual replacement for the card catalog. Present imperfections are only a delay. No phase of library automation excites me more than the potential of unlimited instant printout, index-bibliographies to any portion of the collection, to any topic, and with many more analytics or descriptors for each item than the standard five analytics on cards. In embryo, such cataloging can be found at a number of colleges and universities now, like Florida Atlantic, Louisiana State at New Orleans, Missouri. And as for classification we may yet justify observations by some foreign librarians that expensive L.C. reclassification was unnecessary when the computer works better with a simple I.D. number.

Besides the generic book stock, the Library-College Library will accomodate people. These will include students, faculty and staff. For students, the first departure will be upping the per cent of student body seated at one time from conservative 25%, beyond generous 50%, to 100%. This has been done at Oklahoma Christian, where at present it is 110%. There will be an individual carrel for each student, his individual work bench to which he can come any time of the long day and night the library is open. This does not prevent the student from studying in his own room, if he prefers, with the radio on, or a conversation in progress between his roommate and a dropper-in; or in the play room with every other sentence punctuated by a popping ping pong. But he will also begin to live like he will after he leaves college and has a place of work to report to daily. Nor will this prove architecturally uneconomical when reckoned against unused class space-time.

Faculty offices, one for each faculty member will be in the library. This should stir some librarian opposition based on previous experiences. But recall, please, the learning mode was not that of the Library-College. And for each four faculty offices there should be one seminar room. Faculty offices will be used for study, conference with colleagues and students.

Most of the special areas provided in libraries will be represented: public catalog and bibliography-index area; reference; current periodical; browsing; rare materials; exhibit and display, Equipment storage for projectors, recorders, playbacks, readers, etc, for use with the related formats of the generic book, as well as maintenance and service space areas will be planned. Laboratory and demonstration space will be provided, although the Purdue experiment with biological laboratory may point the ideal accomodation for laboratory in a library.[15]

THE FACULTY

The new breed faculty that will be required for the Library-College is a cross between those librarians who like to teach, and those classroom instructors who like to use the library in their teaching. There are enough of both today to provide a nucleus for the faculty of tomorrow's prototype. Essentially, this faculty member's job will be to guide bibliographically the great adventure in learning by the student. Inspirationally, the faculty member will arouse, through about a half dozen carefully prepared lectures of such significance as to be worthy of public billing on the campus. He will stimulate by stirring seminar discussion, through individual or small group conferences. Bibliographically, he will attempt to tailor media selection to the individual differences of his students, prescribing much as the skilled medical diagnostician.

To accomplish this last, the faculty member will have to know media, not incidentally as he was taught them in his liberal arts or teachers college days, but *per se.* He will have to know his sources not alone for subject but for level. And above all he will have to know the strengths and weaknesses of the various formats for individual learning situations. For example, time-lapse motion pictures can accomplish communication of certain concepts better than almost any other medium. Yet there are some abstractions that cannot be mastered except by wrestling with the printed word. How better can a youngster gather the nuance of Spanish idiomatic conversation than through tape exchanges with college students in Latin American countries.

The time is coming when college orientation and teaching in library use will assume a new importance. With that will come a more creative approach to communicating this important half of knowledge—knowing where to find it. For the present, in-service education is called for. One device is for the faculty to undertake continuous indexing of library materials for computerized retrieval much as is now carried on in scientific libraries. A thesaurus of descriptors, fields, and groups, based on units and terms in the curriculum, could be used as a basis. And the librarian could lead the way by establishing a college interest profile related to faculty research, to specialist and hobby interests.

Prophetically, Carter Alexander anticipated the role of the faculty is this new and more exciting relationship to the student when he wrote:

> "A plan must be developed . . . where the teaching process can be started and finished by the instructor and the learning process carried on effectively in the library . . . where suggestions can be given in the library as well as in the office of the professor."[16]

CURRICULUM

"The curriculum is commonly defined," says the *Encyclopedia of Educational Research,* "as all the experiences that a learner has under the guidance of the school."[17] Although the Library-College accents intellectual development in the library, it by no means neglects "the effects upon learners of all aspects of the community, the home and the school." The Library-College will periodically invite student diaries for review and exchange with the purpose of encouraging students to revise continuously the total experiences planned.

Of the many statements of a liberal education aim, perhaps none will fit the purpose of the Library-College better than this by Professor Richardson to the President of Dartmouth College:

> ". . . the stimulation and development of those gifts of intellect with which nature has endowed the student, so that he becomes, first, a better companion to himself through life, and, second, a more efficient force in his contacts with his fellow men."[18]

To accomplish this purpose the Library-College departs from the curriculum of many contemporary liberal arts colleges by: 1) intellectually accenting general background more, and specialism less; 2) physically and spiritually, converting elements of college life formerly looked upon as "extra" or "co" curriculum to an integral part of the curriculum.

The college curriculum today suffers from the compartmentalization enforced by the predatory rights and privileges of our contemporary academic disciplines. The Library-College will have to recognize these subject areas for some time to come; but it can more solidly develop the student's general background on which to build a specialism by including in its curriculum two "generalia" areas, both in the beginning and as a capstone. One of these areas is "the half of knowledge," that is, "knowing where to find it." It is an area devoted to the study of media, to sources of information, *per se,* done with a dimension and imagination not yet accomplished by our one-hour courses on the use of the library, or certainly by our freshman orientation week. One possible approach is the continuous building of a student-interest profile, covering the range of interests of the student population, and becoming a continuous printout catalog. The student would pursue this course in the Library-College learning mode, working independently under the bibliographic guidance of the instructor.

The other area of "Generalia" would simply be called "Knowledge," for want of a better title at the moment. It would be an overview or summary of the wisdom of mankind; of the thought, actions, and achievements that have most significantly been responsible for man's present state. A beginning might be made through the "Good Books," a collection like that of Harvard President Eliot's the *Harvard Classics,* or Chicago President Hutchins' *Great Books,* if we could eliminate the provincialism of the latter and add the classics of the Eastern World. The student would be encouraged to read across boundary lines, not only within the sciences, the social sciences and the humanities, as our now "old hat" integrated courses do in most colleges, but across these broad areas, so that C.P. Snow's doubtful accusation against the humanists might never be thought again of a college graduate.

On the physical side, the Library-College proposes to include without apology in its curriculum, how to make a living, how to perform in the world, how to get along with his fellow men. Without particularizing further here, the Library-College curriculum has a place for such sacriligious subjects (in the opinion of the intellectualists) as marriage and the family, infant care; the dance-ballroom, go go, and ballet; intercollegiate football; farming; carpentry, etc.

And on the spiritual side, there must be time for meditation. "Where the action is" apparently sells commercially. But if this nation is to be great it must begin to balance our national mind with more contemplation, with time to consider the ultimates. The other day I discovered tucked away in the New Orleans airport a room for meditation. All of us know the famous meditation room in the United Nations. Meditation must be provided for and encouraged in our Library-College, even if it does not involve worship of God. There is no thinking agnostic or atheist I know who does not welcome an opportunity to consider introspectively his decision.

FACILITY

The Library-College does not consider that the last word in library architecture has yet been written. In 1930 I introduced or reintroduced with architect Henry Hibbs, for Fisk University in Nashville, of which I was librarian at the time, the tower stack. The next fashion that followed was probably modular construction. As one who has been frustrated by the fixed columns of the module, and has questioned the advantages of "flexibility" and the uneconomical, reenforced floors throughout, I hope this architectural fashion will at least be critically reexamined by Library-College building planners.

In my opinion, fixed stack for the varied formats of our generic book now seem more justified than ever. Storage for films and hard covers is not practically interchangeable. Nor will the space for projectors lend itself economically to conversions, frequently. As the moment I favor a fixed allotment for the bulk of stock accomodation. As far as possible, media which depend on equipment for use should be placed in proximity to their equipment; at least until remote access is feasible.

Reader accomodation departs from college library building standards, quantitatively by specifying 100% of the student body to be seated at one time. Qualitatively, the individual carrel rather than the group reading table becomes standard. Typical designs for these carrels are available in such publications as the EFL booklet.

Staff accommodation must now provide offices for the new-breed faculty; seminar rooms; and auxiliary bibliographic, browsing, reference, special format, rare, and other work areas. Since the professional librarian will have merged with the classroom instructor to become the faculty, there will still be need to accommodate the management and housekeeping staff, probably according to the "100-foot per," standard.

ORGANIZATION

For the Library-College to function properly its enrollment should be limited to under 500. As enrollments increase on a campus, another college should be organized. For the cluster of colleges, the university should perform certain resources and evaluation functions. Research and other expensive resources which can be shared by all of the colleges will be housed in the university library. All-university lectures by nationally and internationally distinguished scholars will be open to all of the colleges The university will act as an evaluation agency for the programs of the various colleges, each of which may have different accents. A federation of Library-Colleges, therefore, becomes a Library-University.

CONCLUSION

The report of the president of the Carnegie Corporation for

the year ending September 30, 1931 contains these words: Whether the liberal arts college can continue to be "the characteristic element in American life which it has been in the past will probably depend more than anything else upon the colleges themselves. They must demonstrate anew the capacity to produce the men and women whose influence in the world they will enter after graduation can never be measured by mere numbers. This the college succeeded in doing in the past, and can do again in the future, but not by repeating the old techniques, for the world of tomorrow will be a very different place from the world today. As one element in meeting these conditions, the library must be actively and intelligently used by students . . ."

I submit that the Library-College is designed to meet precisely this challenge of preparing a generation for tomorrow.

REFERENCES

1. U.S. Bureau of Education. *College Libraries as Aids to Instruction.* 1880. p. 8-9. (Circulars of Information, No. 1)
2. Brooks, R. C. *Reading for Honors at Swarthmore.* 1927. p. 36.
3. Cutten, G. B. "The Preuptorial System at Colgate University," *Association of American Colleges Bulletin.* 1935. V. 21, p. 493-95.
4. Johnson, B. L., *Vitalizing the College Library.*
5. Harvard
6. The Vespassiano Memoirs (Lives of Illustrious Men of the XVth Century); by Vespassiano de Bisticci, Bookseller: Now first translated into English by William George and Emily Waters. Lincoln Mac Veigh, 19. p. 104.
7. Branscomb, Harvie. *Teaching With Books*; a study of college libraries. 1940. p. 9-10.
8. Shores, Louis. "The Library Arts College." *School and Society*, 1935. V. 61, p. 110-14. (also in *The Library-College*, 1966. p. 3-9) as well as in several anthologies.
9. *Experimental Colleges*; their Role in American Higher Education; ed. by W. High Stickler. 1944. 185.
10. Duffus, R. L. Democracy Enters College. 1936. p. 205.
11. Bennington College, Announcement for the First Year, 1932-33. 1932. (Publications, V.1, Series No. 9, August 1932, No. 1, Part 4)
12. Jennings, F. G. *This Is Reading.* 1965. p. 11.
13. Sutherland, "The College Game is Best." *Sports Illustrated.*
14. Shores, Louis. *Instructional Materials.* 1960.
15. Purdue Lab Experiment
16. Alexander Carter. "The Library Professor and Educational Research," *School and Society*, 1934. V. 39, p. 457-69.
17. Kearney, N. C. and Cook, W. W. "Curriculum," (In *Encyclopedia of Educational Research.* 1960. p. 358-63.

18. Richardson, L. B. A Study of the Liberal College; a report to the president of Dartmouth College. 1924. p. 17.
19. Educational Facilities Laboratory. *Carrels.*

4.

THE TRUE UNIVERSITY . . .

(Essay for the dedication of the new library at Stetson University, DeLand, Florida, and in recognition of Charlotte Smith's 30 years of distinguished librarianship)

IN SEPTEMBER 1974 nearly every American of Freshman age will be trying to go to college. Most of them will apply to junior colleges close to home. The next greatest number will be lining up for admission to their state universities and colleges. Those who can, of the rest of the young people, will be enrolled in private colleges. The United States, as soon as five years from now, will be embarked upon the noble course of providing all of its people with not only an education, but with a *higher* education. History records that no other nation in the world, before or now, has done as much. Those of us who believe universal higher education will bring better understanding between leaders and followers, and thus a more creative society, want this stately commitment to succeed.

But there are hazards ahead. Before another Rickover comes along with a bestselling "What's Wrong with American Higher Education" it behooves us to anticipate such events

The first of these hazards is numbers. If present organizational patterns persist the total student body will continue to be handled in mass. Every registration period young people line up to be treated like so many ID numbers. The so-called required courses with captive classes rival Oklahoma Sooner conditions as lower classmen scramble to register before the "standing room only" signs appear. For other courses, students shop supermarket fashion, heeding fraternity brothers about reputations. "He's stiff," or if you need an "A" to bring your quality points up, here's a crib. As an effort to counsel is made by the administration, the situation improves, but by the very nature of present campus organization advice tends to be "by the number."

A second hazard is in the present evaluation of learning. The standard measure of higher education is the *classroom contact.* When the student receives a bachelor's degree and has a transcript he has evidence that he has been higher educated.

Class contacts, depending upon the concentration of the student and the consecration of the instructor are expected to stir incentive, flash a bit of inspiration, reinforce some stern reading, perhaps even to point the way for further search and exploration, and with none of these purposes can there by any difference. Only the timing comes into question. Should these contacts precede, follow, or coincide with independent study? Is it necessary to meet precisely at nine every Monday, Wednesday, Friday, or could one of these meetings or all of them be dispensed with and another form and calendar of faculty-study relations be established, one tuned to the individual rhythms of differing human beings?

Evidently, some of these hazards and questions are concerning campuses. In the spring of 1964 at Wakulla Springs, Florida State University invited ten experimenting colleges and universities to share their innovations. From Michigan came representatives of three state universities: Michigan to report on its Dearborn, Michigan State on its Oakland, Wayne State on its Monteith. Here were universities, each with upward of 25,000 students, moving to create innovating campuses and small colleges. From California came two educators, one from the new state university at Santa Cruz planned for 27,500 students to be taught in small colleges; the other from the private University of Pacific, already operating as a cluster of small colleges. All five of these universities, moving toward individualizing instruction, were concurrently replacing classroom contacts with independent study or honors reading.

Five small colleges displayed models of independent study almost completely freed from class contacts. Antioch, long famous for its "autonomous courses" gave evidence of heavy reliance on library reading. Stephens, the junior college for women that for many years centered its learning in a "vitalized" library, had more recently augmented the hard cover with a range of "resources" from tape through long-distance telephone that brought famous voices out of Congress in session into student assembly. There was Parsons in Iowa which had declared any college can educate the gifted; send us the rejects. And then there were two new Florida colleges, one—Florida Presbyterian in St. Petersburg, which in four years had selected a library and proceeded to illustrate the power of library learning by compelling the suspension of classes for one whole month each January to insure uninterrupted reading; and New College in Sarasota, still in the dreaming stage, still to prove that it would turn its back on the "class contact" measure of a student's learning, break with the subject specialist's segmented approach, and probe deeper into the library art by enlisting a faculty of teacher-librarians and librarian-teachers. And finally, host Florida State University revealed a proposal for a prototype college of 500 students which, if demonstrated successful, might, within five years, have 25 replicas on a campus of 15,000 students. The prototype would center its academic life in the library, make reading the central learning activity, offer the heterogeneous student a new breed faculty member, a bibliographically committed counselor.

So at Wakulla Springs, eleven American higher educational institutions offered these solutions: Reorganization, no matter how large the student body, into small manageable college units; abandonment of the teacher-centered class contact as the mode of learning in favor of student-centered library reading as a basis for individual independent study.

It has taken academic librarians a long time to see the opportunity and challenge in this trend. To most of us, independent study means, at the utmost more library money, to buy more books, to hire more staff. It suggests that we must improve our service to faculty and students. But this improvement, primarily, means inducing more faculty attention to book selection and use; to speeding our technical processes so that faculty orders will be shelved and cataloged more promptly.

The faculty members who use the library are our strongest allies in gaining support for library appropriation, material, personnel. But above all they most nearly approach our concept of proper teaching and learning. As long as we contend for our ancillary retriever position the most we can hope to do is encourage as many of our colleagues as possible to rely less on classroom contact and more on library reading in student education.

But let us speculate what would happen where the entire faculty consisted of librarians committed to a primary rather than an ancillary role in education. These librarians could be former classroom instructors who were "library oriented" and had increased their bibliographic competence informally or through a formal program in library science; or they could be librarians who had abandoned their ancillary complex and relegated their housekeeping and retriever duties to the subordinate place of ways and means. Actually, the line between so-called classroom and library faculty would be erased and there would be no artificial basis for establishing status as in many institutions today because one teaches in a classroom rather than in a library.

Let us suppose, further, that in this academic community the only educational building is the library, and that the collection includes all formats of the generic term book—hard cover, paperback, celluloid film, rubber disc, magnetic tape, radio or television wave, computerized or manual learning program. The library annex includes laboratories, studios, shops, conference rooms, seminars, classrooms, auditorium, and gymnasium. This complex of campus learning facilities will be called The Library; that is the true university of these days.

Among these books will be all the good and great ones. *The Harvard Classics,* the *Chicago Great Books* and not over 50,000 titles in hard cover and paperback, newspaper and magazine, serial and government publication, map and globe, picture and object, disc and tape, radio and TV program, in representations of all formats. Only the number of titles will be static, for every new title added an old title must be discarded.

Next to the Good Books in importance is a careful selection of Reference Books. With R. books, librarians and library-minded classroom instructors can teach the half of knowledge—where to find it. With R books, too, a beginning can be made in pursuit of the other half—the synthesis and interpretation of knowledge.

Complementary to the Good and to the Reference books will be found a kaleidoscopic selection of other subjects and other forms of material. Music will be represented by phono discs and tapes; art by paintings and photos, sculptures and architectural models, by transparency and opaque projection. Language and literature will be implemented by listening post and audio laboratory utilizing the latest transmission facilities to convert some student carrels into "stations." Professors' lectures will be canned for transmission only when considered worthy of replacing an older "lecture" already available in hard covers.

Now let us make the biggest supposition of all. There are no subjects, courses, class contacts as we now know them. The basic learning activity is reading. Reading may be broad in overview subjects like history, philosophy, man, the cosmos, communications; or narrow on topics like Napoleon, Existentialism, the nervous system, incunabula, or may cut across several subjects and topics near or far apart, not only as in our integrated courses like physical science where we interrelate chemistry, physics, geology, meteorology and mathematics, but as if there were a real unity to the universe and therefore appropriate to seek for relationships between chemistry and music and among such topics as magnetism, chiaroscuro, and demography. In short, through library reading the student would be offered the opportunity to synthesize knowledge, to provide for himself a gestalt of the many compartments into which academic man has divided the universe.

What I am doing is amplifying the original Carlyle quotation. Since the library's collection of books represents a significant summary of man's knowledge, it is the only true curriculum for learning. Rather than constructing a curriculum first and then buying books to support it the true-university first selects a good library and then lets the curriculum follow it. Instead of scheduling classes regularly in circumstcribed subjects and assigning readings in the library irregularly, or not at all, reading is regular; group meetings voluntary, as students feel a need to confer about their library work.

Perhaps the nearest thing to the present regular class contacts will occur in the "Half of Knowledge, knowing where to find it." Rather systematically the librarian will teach by word of mouth, through demonstration, through audio and visual media the use of books and libraries. But this instruction will be done from a perspective far different from that which often renders today's one-hour course in library use impotent. It will be an exciting adventure in searching man's record of thought and deed in order to solve some riddles of the universe.

To bring this "True University" into being we will have to begin with a reconstructed faculty. The individual faculty member will become a cross between today's most educationally-minded librarian and most library-minded clasroom instructor. The latter will be one who does not consider his specialty substantive and the library art of knowing where and overviewing knowledge a sort of intellectual slumming. The former will be happy to be relieved of most of the housekeeping and retriever routines of which so many librarians have made a national holiday. He will be challenged to assume the educational role so long denied him. With these two basic teaching functions of "finding where" and overviewing knowledge the new library faculty can achieve what the old classroom faculty could not—a True University.

A look at the experimenting colleges suggests Carlyle's True University has all but arrived. All that is needed is the courage for a university to declare that it is a community of independent study, of reading students under the guidance of a library faculty with a well-selected book collection. This is a True University dedicated to the higher education of all the people. This University commits itself above all to becoming a great library, so that it may communicate individually to its students "the diary of the human race."

5.

LIBRARY-COLLEGE U.S.A.

(Essay for the Colloquium, Atlanta University School of Library Service faculty and students, to which were invited, also, the faculty and students of the Emory University Division of Librarianship, and librarians of Atlanta libraries, April 2, 1969. Reprinted from *ALA Bulletin* December 1969, 63:1547-53.)

CURRENT CAMPUS unrest has intellectual cause. But those who lead the revolt, today, are not communicating intellectually. They are demonstrating physically *against*; rarely, intelligently *for*. They identify problems *ad nauseam*; almost never, solutions. Their stance is, "tear down first; worry about the build up later." If the so-called Establishment has resisted reform; the Demonstration, now is preventing it. Really, there is little constructive to choose from either party line; and those who march now delay progress as much as those who sit on their predatory advantages. The time has come for positive reform of American higher education.

Let's face it. To be opposed to something is much easier than to be for an idea. Everybody, these days, likes to identify problems. Considering that man is basically imperfect, it's no great trick to discover something is rotten in Denmark. But to correct it so that the correction is better than what we have—ah, as Shakespeare might have said, "That is the rub."

Well, I propose to stick my neck out this afternoon. Contrary to the contemporary mode, I shall devote only one page to summarizing what I think is wrong with American higher education today and the rest of this paper to describing an idea for a prototype education in the first nation to have the courage to college educate every one. I prefer to enter into conversation with students who would rather think than march; with faculty who respond to dialog; with Town people who want to be heard and are willing, reciprocally, to hear Gown people. I want an end to disorder; and a beginning toward orderly, intellectual solutions of our problems.

I appeal to all of my colleagues on the campuses of America to show the way. From history, we know that every action has an equal and opposite reaction. Disorders such as we have been experiencing are an inevitable prelude to distatorship. I never believed before that George Orwell's *1984* could ever happen in America. I fear very much, now, that it may result, unless we who are in higher education take the lead, return to an intellectual form of communication; march less and think more.

And so I begin the hazardous step of offering a solution. Only to satisfy the folklore of the scientific method, I first identify what I consider to be the just intellectual causes for campus unrest. (My students know that I have always believed in identifying solutions first; problems later. But I have always been a radical, not only to the Establishment; but to the Demonstration. I can't stand either one of these party lines. I think the time has come for a *Third Theme* that rejects the realism and pessimism from which both sides suffer.)

The first cause of campus unrest, in my opinion, stems from the noble effort of the United States to college educate every one. Because we have, now, so-called multiversities, with enrollments that have begun to pass the 50,000 mark, higher education has tended to become *impersonal.* Just walk into the gymnasium on registration day on any of our state institutions campuses and observe the frustrations in the long lines, as class sections are announced closed. At the very top of the recent student poll was dissatisfaction with the growing impersonality of higher education. Even the smaller colleges have begun to suffer from the rage to computerize student relations.

Out of this impersonality, caused by numbers, and the trend to "college for all." has come the second justified cause for campus unrest. It relates to the learning mode. When college was restricted to the top 10%, the range of individual differences was narrow enough for the professor to teach with one lecture. But now, with nearly 100% of the high school graduated entering college, classroom teaching, as we have known it, has become impossible. The range of individual differences is so wide that the so-called average presentation bores the gifted, frustrates the underdeveloped, and even discourages the largest center of the bell-shaped curve that higher education has ever known. Classroom-centered teaching, and the class contact as a measure of education have become antiquated. No wonder the present learning mode is referred to, more frequently than ever, as the "Lock-step." We can understand why Emory faculty and students are exultant over their "Wonderful Wednesday," the one day in the week when no classes are permitted.

Add to *Impersonality*, and the *Lockstep*, the *Curriculum* as a third legitimate and intellectual cause for campus disaffection. We call it "liberal," but is it? The Establishment, too, make no mistake, insists on a divine understanding of the meaning of the term. Furthermore, as in Orwell's *Animal Farm*, some subjects are more liberal than others. There is a hierarchy of disciplines. Right now the natural sciences ride the roost. The physical sciences, probably have a little more blue blood than "Bi-sci." But both of them are way above the Social Sciences, despite the fact that the latter have now almost completely subjected themselves to the quantitative, sensory approach to reality that is the *sine qua non* of science's sacred method. Some of these social sciences are more respectable than others. Political Science and Economics rank higher, in the academic blue book, than Sociology; and as for Education, it still belongs on the other side of the railroad track.

The Humanities still have a certain amount of curriculum respect, the kind that is accorded the very old generation, just before they enter the grave. To get back into the action, and especially to get some of Uncle Sam's lush grants, literature and art, music and philosophy, and even theology, which used to top the "liberal" curriculum in the middle ages, are computerizing like mad; trying to out-science science itself. If you want proof of how wrong C. P. Snow is in his essay about "two cultures," look at our single culture academic curriculum. See how totalitarianism can be made to appear liberal. Understand why the curriculum that students have to study, and that faculty have to teach to achieve the status of a bachelor's degree is a third cause of intellectual discontent.

There are other causes of dissatisfaction, too, on our campuses. But these three—Impersonality in teacher-student relations; Lockstep in learning mode; Authorianism in curriculum—I consider fundamental. And for the solution of these three problems I now present to you the concept of Library-College USA.

When a college is a library and a library is a college it is a *Library-College*, spelled with a hyphen between the two words. Bob Jordan has been good enough to attribute the idea to the paper I read before the Chicago World's Fair A.L.A. convention, titled "The Library Arts College." But I acknowledge my debt to Thomas Carlyle and his volume of essays published in 1848, *Hero and Hero Worship*. In the essay "The Hero As Intellectual" occur these often quoted words:

The true university is a collection of books.

What is not as often cited is the context. Carlyle's point is that there is very little more that a professor can do for a student than teach him how to read intelligently. After that, the student is on his own. What he learns he will have to study independently. Nobody can learn for him.

Independent study by the student is the very essence of the Library College learning mode. In the last analysis, it is the student who must struggle with his environment, master its obstacles to his purpose. A steady recognition of this basic learning principle is permeating innovation in higher education over these United States. At least 100 experimental colleges report variations on the independent study theme. Antioch began with what they called autonomous courses, as early as 1928. My visit to an economics class there that September gave me an early impetus for the Library-College idea.

Florida Presbyterian has a winter term during the month of January when there are no classes; all students study independently in the library. I have already mentioned Emory's "Wonderful Wednesday," when there are no classes. But Emory has demonstrated something else, in the only kind of demonstration that communicates with me. Many colleges have insisted that independent study is only for the honors student; the elite. On the contrary. Emory has proved this learning mode is especially made to order for the underdeveloped student, and for the majority we like to call average. All over the country, now, you hear of more colleges turning to *independent study in the library* as the prime learning mode; with the classroom becoming secondary experience. This is so, because the student's ability to study on his own is the real payoff. As Winslow Hatch puts it in his "New Dimensions" pamphlet for the U.S. Office of Education, one of the measures of quality education is the degree to which a student can study independently. Colleges which have turned to independent study are along the Library-College way.

All the professor can do in preparation for independent study is, as Carlyle wrote, over a century ago, teach the student how to read intelligently. Indeed, this has been the heart of higher learning at Oxford and Cambridge, and at the great universities on the continent. When I was in England on my Fulbright year I never heard any one say he was enrolled in a course in history, or economics, or physics, or French. What I heard, always, was "He is *reading* in history at Oxford; he is *reading* in Physics at Cambridge; she is *Reading* in French at the Sorbonne."

However, by reading, we of the Library-College mean more than just reading the printed page in hard covers. This is still basic. But it isn't all. Some of you who have read my pleading writings on this, know about my concept of the *Generic Book*. You know of my long struggle to effect, what some have referred to as the "shotgun marriage" between librarians and audiovisualists. My students know that the term "Non-book" is anathema to me. There is no such term in my vocabulary. A film is a book, just as truly as a magazine. So is a tape or a transparency; a radio transcription or a videotape; a teaching machine of programmed materials; or a field trip to the phosphate mine; an interview with an old resident; or a computer-assisted instructional device. As I defined the *Generic Book* in my *Saturday Review* editorial for the first National Library Week, it is *the sum total of man's communication possibilities*. The *Generic Book*, in all of its formats, levels and subjects, represents the only evidence of life. And that philosophical concept I advance here, although among the oh-so-liberated librarians among us, librarians are not supposed to be philosophical; nor are we capable of writing good literature; and of course, library school, according to the writers of letters to the editor of the *Library Journal*, is supposed to be the worst education of all.

Forgive me. I am an optimist. I believe our profession of librarianship is the noblest of them all. I'll stack our library literature, for form or content, up against the literature of any other discipline or profession, and I prefer it to the novels and plays that are coining money, with four-letter words, these days. And as for Library School, I have seen more good teaching and learning in our ALA accredited schools, than in most of the graduate school classes in other disciplines I have visited.

Let me return, then, to reading, and the generic book, which are the heart of the Library-College idea. Independent Study requires that the student be able to read the generic book in all of its formats. As Frank Jennings writes in his little gem of a book, *This is Reading,*

> "But reading, remember, is not restricted to the printed page. Actually it never was . . . throughout his history man has 'read' many things: the flight of birds, the guts of sheep, sun spots, liver spots and the life lines on a hand. He has read the lore of the jungle, the spoor of the beast and the portents in a dish of tea . . ." (1965, p.11)

And just as man has read many things, throughout the ages, so the Library-College student must learn to see and hear, to taste, smell, and touch, indeed, increasingly, to extrasense, communication with his environment, with fellow man, and with God, or with whatever ultimate you recognize exists.

So the Lirary-College becomes first of all a true university as Carlyle defined it—a collection of books that comprise a selection of the generic book. This selection is no longer a collection of hard cover print and periodicals, with some so-called audiovisuals added on as a concession. The Library-College library approaches selection, from the start, on a three-prong basis: *subject,* as now: *level* of maturity of the community served, as sometimes currently considered in academic librarianship; *format,* as almost never weighed from the standpoint of the 100 or more forms of the generic book now available.

In my book *Instructional Materials,* I tried, for the first time to present a format classification of the generic book. Beginning with Print, I overviewed the literature in the subforms of textbook, reference book, reading book, serial, etc. But I did not stop there, as so often conventional library book selection does. I proceeded with Graphics, taking the literature of such subforms as maps, pictures, objects, etc.; then to Projections, with the subforms of slides, filmstrips, transparencies, miniatures, and motion pictures; to Transmissions, like discs and tapes, radio and tv; through community resources; and machines and computer media.

Why is this important to independent study, the learning mode of the Library-College? Because, for the first time in the history of education the quantity and variety of media provide a range of individual differences that can match the individual differences of students. It is no longer necessary to communicate with an average lesson plan in a classroom. It is now possible to tailor the message to the individual, to realize, at long last, the dream of the pedagogue to individualize instruction.

And in this, make no mistake, format is at least as important a consideration as subject and level. Through all of the histronics that has brought Marshall McLuhan more salary and more celebrity than any college professor in the history of higher education, one significant educational principle has been reenforced. The format of a medium, that is the physical makeup of it, may influence the individual learning situation. Thus, one student may understand better a specific idea from a printed page; another student by way of a tv videotape; a third through a field trip to a community resource; a fourth at a remote computer console. This makes it imperative in the Library-College library that book selection, become *generic book* selection; that student and faculty interest profiles are studied; and that selective dissemination of information, what the information scientist has most recently reawakened us to, is practiced.

Do you begin to see the Library-College approach to learning? Every student, from his first Freshman day is moved forward, from the dependence his high school classroom teaching days may have imposed, to increasing independence. He is provided the environment of independence from the start. For example, we used to think that if a library could seat 25% of the student body at one time, it was generously meeting standards. But think of Oklahoma Christian College, one of those innovative institutions I mentioned earlier. It can seat *110%* of its student body at one time, and each student with his exclusive "wet" carrel. How wet? At the moment, students have dial access, at their individual carrels, to a limited range of formats: tapes, discs, and possibly some visuals. Before long, they will have LDX, long distance xeroxing that will reproduce print or visuals; and they will have tv, radio, canned lectures, and a wider range of the formats of the generic book.

I do not mean to overemphasize hardware. This is our American weakness. I would rather say something of the software, and of the philosophical concepts behind the Library-College idea. None of these technological spectaculars will be worth their expense unless they have a purpose. The basic ends are to personalize and individualize education; to come up with a curriculum that will be more meaningful to the next generation, and enable this generation to cope with the revolt their children will inevitably confront them with.

Make no mistake about that. Today we have a lot of middle-aged demagogues who go about proclaiming to the hippie minority such platitudes as "you have inherited problems you did not create." As if this could not have been said to every other young generation that has ever appeared on this planet. But I dare these demagogues to say to the hippie, I am positive your generation will present absolutely no problems to your children. I'd like to bet that the hippies' children will shave their heads; score the beat; come up with a love-out; or a hate-in; call the older generation "rounds;" and tell them to "freeze, adolescent, freeze."

The Library-College personalizes education, first, by its organization. No matter how large a campus grows, intimate faculty-student communication will continue. And the Library-College campuses will grow, because the Library-College is committed to universal higher education. It believes every high school graduate is higher educable. To protect faculty-student intimacy, no Library-College has as many as a thousand students; and preferably serves under 500. As enrollment grows, new Library-Colleges are activated, so that United States University looks more like the British cluster-college campus. Already, the trend to this organizational pattern has begun. The University of California at Santa Cruz, for example, though it may ultimately have nearly 30,000 students, will have no one college on its campus with as many as 1,000 students.

Second, the Library-College breaks the lock-step in higher education's current classroom-centered teaching by insisting on a carrel-centered independent study learning mode. Students work at their exclusive workbenches, dialed for access to a range of media formats, levels and subjects. Independent study is regular; class meetings irregular, and only when students feel a need for group meetings.

A new breed faculty, a sort of cross between today's library-minded teacher, and teaching-minded librarian, lectures less, and guides more, bibliographically. The professor in the Library-College has a sensitive art that enables him to match individual differences in students with individual differences in media. To be able to do this, he must not only know his students, probably better than most of us do now, but he must know his media, as he certainly does not now. As far back as 1940, Chancellor Emeritus Harvie Branscomb pointed out in his classic study of American college faculties, done for the Carnegie Corporation, that the average professor teaches inadequately with books and libraries because he does not know them.

There is still a place for the lecture, and speech communication is also part of the generic book. But freed from the deadly necessity of meeting class regularly, the professor will no longer feel compelled to pre-digest for the students information available in other media for independent study. Rather, the faculty can contribute original work, at all-university lectures, of such calibre as to warrant publication or production.

There are, also, a share of devices for learning in the Library-College, some lost in the history of education, and others quite innovative. For example, in the 18th century, Bell and Lancaster introduced something called the monitorial system, under which each advanced student had responsibility for tutoring a beginning student. Every teacher knows that he learned more about his subject the first time he had to teach it to someone, than in all of the time he studied it for himself. This device has recently been revived in the world literacy effort of Dr. Laubach. It is an integral part of the Library-College learning mode.

Performance is an important aspect of Library-College education. Not only speaking and writing, but performance in at least one of the fine arts is underwritten. Furthermore, the Library-College erases the artificial line that academic snobbery sometimes draws between living and making a living. The Library-College includes occupational preparation in its concept of a liberal education. Possibly in cooperation with labor unions and industry, a work-study program is developed to insure for society, higher educated carpenters and plumbers, electricians and masons, etc., who may bring back the pride in workmanship we once celebrated.

Finally, another approach to curriculum development is proposed by the Library-College. Without discounting the importance of heritage, as provided by past generations, (as demonstrators sometimes appear to), the Library-College provides an opportunity for the new generation to test its dissents and reforms. Through the device used by librarianship in other settings, students, from the start, establish their own interest profiles, their preferred curricula. These interests have their place in the Library-College curriculum as significantly as do the faculty interest profiles, and both profiles, faculty and student, are prime considerations in media selection for the Library-College library.

Without detailing the Library-College curriculum here (as it can be found in the book) let me call attention merely to the first two reading areas, the ones I have called *Generalia* Areas. We have gone overboard on specialisms, in my opinion. The Library-College, for the present, transitionally works with the broad organizations of the Humanities, Social Sciences, Natural Sciences, and their applications; but not to the extent that it believes, philosophically, that Genesis should be rewritten in terms of chemistry, economics, literature, and the other disciplines so sacred to the card-carrying union members of the learned societies. But the Library-College believes,fundamentally, in the unity of the universe, and therefore in the unity of knowledge. It believes, what the curriculum needs most, these days, is a *gestalt,* a bringing together of the fiercely separated subjects that confront the college student at different hours of the day.

Hence, the Library-College has a Generalia Area that consists of two parts. The first recognizes the truth of that often quoted statement from the prolific writer Anon: "The half of knowledge is knowing where to find it." A thorough foundation in information gathering is given to each student, so that he knows sources better than even the college faculties of this generation. The Library-College student is given a library sophistication that will fortify him with knowledge in depth about the basic reference books, bibliographic tools, media formats of all kinds. No Library-College student will ever have to admit, like a physics professor did to me not so long ago, that he had never known before of the information mine that has been issued every year for over a century under the title, *The Statesman's Yearbook.*

As for the other half of knowledge, the Library-College offers in its curriculum a broad reading area that skips across the boundary lines of predatory disciplines, recklessly. The Library device of browsing; the eclectic bibliographies, like Chicago President Hutchins' "Great Books of the Western World" and Harvard President Eliot's "Five-Foot Shelf" of the classics of both the western and eastern worlds; and previewing and pre-audings of audio-visual media, provide ready made gateways to a liberal education. A Freshman overview, and a senior capstone insure not only an understanding of relationships among man's disciplines, but offer an opportunity for serendipity, the latest rediscovery by both cultures.

Here you have *Library-College USA*, prototype for an American higher education. Its imperfections are many. It is no panacea for all the campus dissatisfactions. But it is a positive proposal. It is a challenge to some college to try it. And in my opinion it is better than marching.

6.

PROTOTYPE
For an American Higher Education

(Essay for the Library-College Interdisciplinary Conference, LaSalle Hotel, Chicago, November 7, 1969.)

CAMPUS UNREST today is of two kinds. One kind protests negatively; the other kind plans positively. The protesters have captured our media; the planners have been all but ignored by television, and relatively neglected by our press. One of the myths our tv networks, particularly, have tried to promote, is the so-called "generation gap." After a campus lifetime I declare, unequivocally, the *gaps within generations* are greater than the *gaps between generations.*

Look at both Town and Gown. Those who march and demonstrate, in urban and campus disorders, are neither all under, or over, thirty years of age, if that is the chronological boundary line between generations. No 19-year old draft card burner is more melodramatic in his protest against our half of the Vietnam war than is the 66-year old doctor of momism. Bertrand Russell is 97. In universities where the four-letter word has become the symbol of intellectual freedom, the oh-so-liberated co-ed editor of the college *avant gard* monthly magazine is usually encouraged by the English instructor twice her age. Young and old, these generations together denounce something they vaguely define as the "Establishment."

Just as the Demonstration on the campus represents no more than 5% of the students, and no more than 5% of the faculty, so the marchers in our city disorders represent no more than 5% of the melting pot that is the American nation. Those who prefer exhibitionist communication, the "non-violent" violence that has brought fear and force into our way of life, instead of reason and reform, are represented by all ages, faiths, politics, origins, hues. Despite the claims of their leaders, the March has retarded progress toward the good society. The March's greatest achievement to date has been its conquest of our mass media, principally the television networks, because it has succeeded with its histronics in introducing some new dimensions to show business.

The Demonstration has been aided and abetted by what it calls the Establishment, another 5% of our population, of all ages, faiths, politics, origins, hues. Both of these minorities, the Demonstration and the Establishment, are the negative forces in our society. They pride themselves on identifying problems; abhor solutions. In this "establishment" are those who have unearned wealth, or are being over rewarded in relation to their contribution to our society. Their repudiation of the so-called "Puritan Ethic" fortifies the Demonstration in their "love-ins." Mutually, the Demonstration and the Establishment tear down a way of life that comparatively, both today, and in the long history of nations, has done more than ever before to reduce man's imperfections.

The tyranny of these two minorities over the majority of Americans who have made this nation good, even more significantly than great, is one of the saddest commentaries on our time. Uncelebrated by our mass media, and underestimated, particularly by our dangerously powerful television networks, the majority of Americans work hard and creatively. They strive, perhaps mistakenly, to make it easier for their children. Despite the mounting divorce rate, glamorized by our mass media in their glorification of the so-called celebrity, the majority of our marriages still survive. A few couples, perhaps to the disgust of the more sensational communicators, even observe silver and golden anniversaries. For either the Demonstration or the Establishment to call the majority "hypocritical" is the epitome of hypocrisy.

This tyrannizing of the productive majority by the two drone minorities occurring in American society generally, today, appears in its most unjust form on the campuses of some of our so-called multiversities. The protesting *generations together*—students and faculty—comprising no more than 5% of the academic community, have repudiated intellectual communication. They have hypocritically chosen under organizational names that often include the words "democratic action," such undemocratic actions as walking out when the other side comes up to bat; preventing fellow students and faculty from library study; occupying rooms and buildings; and even engaging in open warfare with firearms and arson while protesting our half only of the Vietnam war.

But while these protesters, faculty malcontents, as well as student disrupters, identify problems *ad nauseam*, problems which others always cause, never the protesters, a majority of the students and faculty are going about the main business of an academic community—to study man's imperfect quest for perfection. In libraries, laboratories, and classrooms these generations together identify problems no less vigorously than do the protesters. But the majority do this intellectually rather than physically. Furthermore, they study comparatively, the "establishments" of nations today, and of other times, to discover solutions of the past and the present.

On at least 100 campuses in the United States that I know from a half century of academic life, faculty and students—the generations together—are experimenting and planning innovations that will reform and improve American higher education. It is these generations together to whom CBS referred, unctuously, in its recent "Generations Apart" sereies, as "conformists." When it was suggested to them that in fairness the intellectual efforts at reform by these so-called "conformists" deserved at least one program to balance three for the protesters, the response was that CBS was not concerned with innovation. Even more strangely, that part of the "Establishment" which trades under the name Xerox, and which financed the series on CBS, also found, that when it came to revealing or supporting the positive innovation on our college campuses, the budget had already been committed elsewhere.

So, I use the only medium still available to me to communicate one of these innovations—one that in my partial opinion, is more important to the improvement of American higher education than all of the negative antics of CBS' beloved coiffured gentry. First, let me describe the Library-College movement in general; and then, what Bob Jordan has called the Shores Library-College version.

When a college is a library and a library is a college, it is a Library-College. Note that the term is spelled with a hyphen. The Library-College, most of us agree, is characterized by its learning mode, which reverses the present relation between classroom and library, by making individual, independent study, in a carrel, primary; group teaching in a classroom secondary. Independent study is reenforced by what I call the *generic book,* that is media in all formats, from textbook to television; from magazine to motion picture from reference source to computer-assisted instructional console; from lecture, to laboratory, to field trips, and through all of the countless media formats that comprise print, audiovisual, other sensory, and even extrasensory means of communication. Simply, the *generic book can be defined as the sum total of man's communication possibilities.*

Bob Jordan has generously credited me with the origin of the Library-College idea, based on my paper before the American Library Association World's Fair convention, in Chicago in 1933.[1] I acknowledge my debt to Thomas Carlyle, English essayist of the 19th century, who wrote the often quoted line in his book, *Heroes and Hero Worship*

"The true university these days in a collection of books."[2]

After my 1933 paper, which *School and Society,* first published, and which has been reprinted many times since, the idea rested, until after V-J day, except for one 1940 challenge to the academic world. In that year appeared Chancellor Emeritus Harvie Branscomb's *Teaching With Books,* an educational classic ever since. It was based on an investigation (for the Association of American Colleges, financed by a grant from the Carnegie Corporation) of the educational effectiveness of the college library. Addressed to "college presidents, teachers, librarians, and others responsible for undergraduate education," it revealed, intellectually and intelligently, rather than physically, some defects in our campus efforts.[3]

To the college classroom teacher he said, very frankly indeed, for those days, ". . . knowledge of a large part of nearly every course can be secured not only as well but actually better from two or three standard volumes than from the lectures of the professor." (p.61) For the college president he cited the daring move of President Wood of Stephens College in 1931 when he appointed B. Lamar Johnson to the joint position of librarian and dean of instruction, with these words, "The conception back of this . . . challenges the complacency with which many colleges regard their traditional organization and practice, namely, that the use of books is not an incidental aspect of instruction, but central and primary . . ." (p. 101) And as for the college librarian, Dr. Branscomb dared him to stop being "so imitative of other institutions . . ." and to realize that "the fundamental need of the college library is to develop a distinctive program of its own."

The Library-College movement, I believe, is the most creative response to that challenge that has yet appeared. It accepts not only the challenge to the librarian, but the other two challenges as well—to the college classroom instructor, and to the college president. The growth of the movement since its revival by Robert Jordan, Dan Sillers, Howard Clayton, Sister Helen Sheehan, B. Lamar Johnson, Tom Minder, Theodore Samore, Patricia Knapp, Janice Fusaro, and many more, has been all the more remarkable without the financial and media support given to the negative campus protest. Beginning with a modest newsletter, Library-College Associates, Inc., now publishes an attractive quarterly[4] under the capable editorship of Dr. Howard Clayton of the University of Oklahoma. Several conferences on innovation, including those at Kenyon, Syracuse, and Drexel,[5] which resulted in books, have advanced the movement. Probably as many as 100 experimental and innovative colleges all over the United States now feature elements of the Library-College concept. Interest in the concept has spread abroad, and particularly in the United Kingdom, where Mr. Beswick has written eloquently about the movement.[6]

Although there is general agreement among us on the basic concept that when a college is a library and a library is a college it is a Library-College, there are a number of variations on the application of the theory, and on specific elements. This is abundantly illustrated in the Drexel volume. In recent years, especially in the face of campus unrest, I have modified some of my own designs for this prototype of what I believe American higher education will become in the next few years.

INTIMACY VERSUS IMPERSONALITY

Let me therefore sketch my Library-College against the background of what I consider some of the valid discontents with the shape of higher education in the United States today. At the top of the dissatisfactions listed by students, in some recent polls, is the growing impersonality, especially in what we now call multiversities. All one has to do is visit the gymnasium of a 15,000-plus enrollment institution on registration day to confirm the frustration with the wholesale treatment of young people. The fact that the process has been computerized, only serves to accent psychologically the fact that the student is an ID and that education is by the number. Furthermore, after registration, the student is frequently herded into auditorium classes of 1,000 students, or more, in which any note taking must be done uncomfortably on the lap or on a makeshift writing surface. The professor makes his grand entrance like a symphony orchestra conductor, delivers a rehash of information the student could gather more quickly out of the kind of sophisticated library use he is never taught. Just as grandiosely the lecturer makes his exit, without ever getting to know any of his thousand or more students. If you think this is exaggerated come visit a freshman psychology class with me, which I have listened to bright young men and women describe discouragedly.

But most of my students have had no inclination to protest this educational outrage, physically. They have preferred to study education historically, comparatively, philosophically; to dialogue and document their problems; and to propose solutions to be undertaken, experimentally. Many of these experiments have resulted in innovations of exciting proportions. The 20 colleges that have formed an experimental union, with headquarters at Antioch College, Yellow Springs, Ohio, is an example.[7] Individual junior and senior colleges; universities and professional schools have pioneered higher educational dimensions in independent study, classless terms or days, curriculum concepts, media resources, computerized facilities, teacher-student relations, campus organization.

To meet the problem of impersonality, resulting primarily from the geometric increase in the student population, the Library-College proposes a British, Cambridge-Oxford-like cluster college campus, in which no single college will exceed an enrollment of 600 students, slightly more or less. As many as ten, or even 20, of these colleges may constitute the undergraduate division of a university. Each college indicates its independence in individual facility, faculty, student body, curriculum accent, etc. But every college, also, shares in the common, greater facility, faculty, student bodies, curriculum accents, etc. of the total university.

THE LEARNINNG MODE

As objectionable as the growing impersonality is the classroom-centered group teaching. It represents a kind of lockstep in which the pace is set for all by a mythical average. Perhaps this group-teaching method was possible when college was restricted to the so-called elite, top 10%. But now, with universal higher education in prospect, the range of individual differences is so wide that a single class presentation not only bores the "gifted" and discourages the "retarded," but fails to provide an aperitif for learning, even for the vast "average." I have placed all three of these terms in quotes because I do not accept them, for reasons I will indicate. Furthermore, higher education in America, today, measures education in terms of numbers of class contacts. The average undergraduate is expected to accumulate about 125 semester hours of class credit as evidence of a bachelor education.

The Library-College shifts the locus of learning from the classroom to the library carrel. In place of group teaching, there is a new learning mode of individual independent study. Under faculty bibliographic guidance the student matches his individual differences with the individual differences found in the range of media formats, levels and subjects that comprise the generic book. The student goes as far as he can on his own, and with his monitor; then with his instructor, in conference; after that in seminar, class, lecture, lab, as groups of students agree with faculty on need.

Elaborating on the Library-College learning mode a bit more as I conceive it: for the first time in the history of education we can now match individual differences in students with individual differences in media. The Generic Book now includes much more than print, although, unlike Marshall McLuhan, I do not underestimate the communication possibility of print. Nor do I overestimate the communicability of television. Indeed I detected a slight look of surprise on Professor McLuhan in his own 16-mm film when it was discovered that children asked to draw from a tv program were more imitative than when asked to draw from a radio program. What Professor McLuhan has succeeded in popularizing is something we who teach have talked our hearts out in vain about—namely, the *format*, as well as the level and subject of media may influence communicability. Now this principle about which I have tried to write in both my books and articles is at the heart of the Library-College learning mode.

Out of this new learning mode is emerging a new breed student and faculty. The student, first, is appearing as an independent, active learner, rather than as a passive note-taker. At his individual work-bench in the library he explores among the media selected for his purpose, jointly with his monitor, his fellow students, and above all with his new-breed instructor. With increasing discrimination he concentrates on those media that communicate with his present background. He browses in print of all types—textbook, reference book, serial, document. But he doesn't stop with print. He searches through a repertoire of multi-splendored graphics—pictures of all kinds, drawings and paintings, photographs in color and black and white, flat and 3-d. Then there is the whole range of charts and graphs, diagrams and pictographs. He looks at murals, and may even help create and produce dioramas. There is a world of what the audiovisualist elegantly refers to as realia, and the librarian calls objects, from natural specimens to man-made models and mockups. All of these are media of unlimited individual differentiation.

But they are only a small part of the generic book. Projected media for example encompass the opaque projection of all of the graphic and print types. Projected media also include a range of transparent materials, from slides to filmstrips, from 10 by 10 transparencies to microtexts. And in the world of sound, there are discs and tapes, radio and television, and their stored and retrieved communications in the form of transcriptions, kinescopes, and videotapes. Through field trips, natural, social, and human resources are communicated less vicariously than in other media formats. And lately, through technology, a whole new media format of programmed instruction has been reenforced by machine and computer.

This is no attempt here to repeat the format classification of media I have detailed elsewhere.[8] It is an effort to suggest what tangibles now make the Library-College mode of independent study more possible than ever before. With the appearance of the wet carrel, so-called, for each student, access to the whole range of media formats, subjects, and levels is within dial access. Excitingly, the day is now almost here when the student can have at his own work bench everything from the tape of the professor's lecture he missed, to a printed page, or a transparency, or a 16mm motion picture, or a micro-projection. He can have repeated for him as often as he chooses a single complex part of a laboratory demonstration.

Will these media replace the human teacher? On the contrary:

without the life and blood of humans the generic book doesn't exist. Remember the Generic Book's definition as the sum total of man's communication possibilities. This includes not only the creation of these media by human beings but their continuous interpretation thereafter. Both the creation and the interpretation are the essence of the Library-College learning mode.

Beginning with the student himself who struggles with the communication a human produced for him, and proceeding to fellow students who dialogue with him as peers, the *human* teaching process is evident. Then comes the Monitor, whom I have borrowed for my Library-College from Bell, and Lancaster, of the 18th century, and from Laubach, of the 20th. As you recall Andrew Bell in Madras and Joseph Lancaster in London developed a monitorial system of education, in which more advanced pupils, under the master's direction tutored and aided less advanced pupils. A contemporary version of this educational concept is illustrated by Dr. Laubach's world literacy crusade in which "each one teaches one." In my Library-College idea, the monitorial system is of mutual advantage to advanced and less advanced student alike.

Over both, the student's independent study and his dialog with fellow students and monitors, are faculty. The new brood teacher knows not only the individual differences of his students, but the generic book so well that he can match individual differences in students with individual differences in media. It is this sensitive guidance that is the heart of the new breed faculty's role in the Library-College. Around this new teaching technique vibrates all the qualities of motivation, and provocation, inspiration and excitement that has ever made the teacher good and great.

PREDATORIES VERSUS PROFILES

Third among students' valid disaffections with higher education is the curriculum of predatory disciplines. The hierarchy of subjects in American higher education today is so exclusive that only a select few may call themselves "liberal." Furthermore, among them some are more liberal than others. Right now the natural sciences are at the very top of respectability, the physical ones perhaps a shade higher than the so-called "bi-scis." Next come the humanities, increasingly furthering their defenses by adopting the sacred method of science in the learning of language and literature, philosophy and religion, and even in the fine arts. As every day goes by, C. P. Snow's two cultures merge into one, and novelists brag of the research that goes into the production of their fiction; musicians turn to electronics, and painters devote themselves more to this world, and less to the next. The social sciences, of course, long ago submitted to the quantitative approach for society, and no history now can hope to be considered unless it is scientific. And as for psychology and education, still struggling for acceptance, there is no question that the only path is the method of the physical sciences.

If the natural sciences, humanities, and social sciences are all accepted as liberal, their applications, like engineering, agriculture, business, homemaking, and athletics are not. It goes without saying that the study of such human graces as etiquette, cosmetics, typing, social secretaryship, fashion, are outside the meaning of "liberal." And, of course, the trades, and the training for any occupation can not be considered as part of a liberal curriculum.

The Library-College differs fundamentally, on this concept of a liberal education. It believes the rigid line drawn between pure-applied, between liberal and vocational is artificial. Education of the whole man, and the whole woman, suggests to the Library-College that liberal education encompasses the whole range of both proximates and ultimates that confront human existence. Consequently, although the Library-College must modulate between the current course of study, and the curriculum for the next generation, the Protoype calls for an immediate crossing of the liberal-vocational boundary line. To some extent, the junior college is spearheading this higher educational revolution; and a few courageous senior colleges and universities are steadily challenging the liberal pre-emptions of the predatory disciplines.

Overall, the Library-College sees the curriculum as a continuous dialog between faculty and students. If humans are not to revert to animals, then the older generation must not abdicate its responsibility to transmit the heritage. It is the faculty's obligation to its students to summarize what it considers of greatest significance to mankind—the noblest deeds and thoughts of men of the past—as well as the concerns and failures, the problems and riddles, of this world and of the universe.

But the students, too, have a role in this curriculum dialog. There is more than an outside possibility, especially if Wordsworth's line, "the child is father to the man" is true, and I believe it is, that the younger generation having come more recently from that mysterious eternity may have a little more of it about him. Consequently, the Library-College faculty, continuously, through a number of devices that both faculty and students may develop, searches for curriculum revisions and innovations. One of these devices, not used adequately, if at all, by the traditional college is what I call the Student Interest Profile. In the form of syllabi, the faculty indicates significances of the past. By listing in rank order his most vital interests at this point, the student indicates his half of the curriculum dialog, and this half is recognized tangibly by the Library-College. In the first place, a considerable portion of the student's independent study in the carrel is devoted to these interests, whether they occur among the predatory disciplines or not. Second, the Library-College Library scelects media as carefully for the Student Interest Profiles as it does for the Faculty syllabi. Finally, all of the human resources from students, monitors and faculties, to outside experts are enlisted equally for both syllabi and profiles.

In addition to avocational interests of students, vocational ones, too, are not co-curricular, but integral to the liberal concept. Consequently, the Library-College insists that every student will have an opportunity to develop all of his interests and talents for recreation and occupation. Because space for detail is running out, the Library-College I advocate recognizes dancing and intercollegiate football as possible liberal disciplines for some students. It also rejects any condescension toward the trades and skills, and maintains that brickmasons, plumbers, homemakers will be even better performers, as well as citizens, with education in history, music, philosophy, etc., and in spiritual and ethical ultimates.

To further the occupational interest of students, as well as to restore to society workers in all of the skills and trades with pride in their work, the Library-College will strive to establish work-study relations with industry, business, agriculture, government, etc. The university which comprises the cluster of Library-Colleges, may even establish some enterprises of its own, like printing and publishing, farm, home maintenance service. The student's academic calendar may alternate on a semi-annual rotation of work-study, or morning-afternoon day, in which two students team.

LIBRARY-COLLEGE GOVERNMENT

A fourth and final element of discontent is academic government. At the heart of the campus protest is the dichotomy fostered by most American colleges and universities. Faculty and students operate separate governments, publications, activities, of one kind or another, far more frequently than they operate them together. It is unthinkable to my idea of a Library-College that there should be anything like a student newspaper, or a faculty bulletin, rather than academic community media of all formate—newspaper, magazine, radio, tv, etc. The fundamental concept of the Library-College is that students and faculty are in this business of education together.

Formally, each Library-College, in a university cluster, might model its governmental structure after one of the 50 states: the university government imitating the structure of our federal government. The bicameral legislatures could consist of a faculty senate and a student house of representatives. Student representation might be elected on class ratios, *e.g.*, freshmen 1:50, sophomores 1:40, juniors 1:30, seniors 1:20, graduate students 1:10. Similar ratios for faculty ranks in the senate might also be established. The executive branch, headed by the dean for a college, by the president for the university, would operate with a cabinet composed of both students and faculty, appointed by the president; all appointments to be confirmed by the faculty-student congress. The courts, joint faculty-student, would adjudicate in many of the injustices and accusations that today result in violence.

But positive efforts at reform would be recognized through a regular day each week in the academic calendar, which I have named *Sotuday*, that is state of the university day. On that day, campus meetings, modeled on the New England Town meeting would be held all over the campus to deliberate on issues, vote and transmit through the instruments of referendum, initiative and recall, needed action to strengthen the academic community. Debate on all sides would be reenforced by library documentation, and intellectual and esthetic communication, including artistic posters and signs, projections of slides, filmstrips, transparencies, radio and tv programs, and orderly election parades.

CONCLUSION

There are many more elements in the Library-College innovation that I should like to describe; but these descriptions will have to wait for my next book, titled *USU*. Here, I wish only to close with a challenge to all those who march, and other wise communicate physically, rather than intellectually: abandon this form of domestic aggression, in the interest of the good society most of us want. Revive the town meeting as a more effective form of communication. Use the instruments provided by the constitutions of the United States and its 50 states, namely, initiative, referendum, recall to bring about needed reforms.

If this form of communication is preferable for town, how much more is this desirable for gown. The campus is an intellectual community. It does not behoove us—students or faculty—to label our actions democratic, when we use force to occupy facilities, and prevent freedom to read, speak, study, for any who do not rubber stamp our position.

I have compared two documents very carefully, one written in 1776 by Thomas Jefferson; the other by Karl Marx and Friedrich Engels in 1848. Although there may be some difference of opinion between the two political divisions of today's world as to which of these two documents is the more revolutionary, the better written, or the more promising for the coming of the good society, there should be no difference on the right of nations and individuals to choose between them as to the course followed in pursuit of reform. All of my librarian reading, and first-hand observation abroad, convince me that Jeffersonian Democracy offers the United States a better way of the good life than does Marxian communism.

I therefore invite my academic colleagues—students and faculty—on campuses all over the United States, to abandon today's physical demonstrations, and to resume intellectual communication, to the end that we may speed the coming of the Prototype for an American higher education.

REFERENCES

1. Shores, Louis. "The Library Arts College." *School and Society*, 1935. 4:110-14.
2. Carlyle, Thomas. *Heroes and Hero Worship*.
3. Branscomb, Harvie, *Teaching With Books*, 1940. p. 239.
4. *The Library-College Quarterly*. Norman, University of Oklahoma, 1968-.

5. Shores, Louis, Jordan, Robert, *et al. The Library-College.* Philadelphia, Drexel Press, 1966.
6. Beswick, The Library-College. London, England, Library Association, 1968.
7. Union of Experimental Colleges. *Bulletins.* Yellow Springs, Ohio, Antioch College.
8. Shores, Louis. *Instructional Materials.* 1960. Chap. 1.

LIBRARY - COLLEGE USA

PART TWO: JUNIOR COLLEGE IMPACTS

7.

THE JUNIOR COLLEGE IMPACT ON ACADEMIC LIBRARIANSHIP

(Essay for the Illinois Library Association, Chicago, October 18, 1968. Published in *College and Research Libraries*, 1969, 30:214-21)

IF I WERE an academic librarian again—university, senior college, or junior college—*Innovation* would be the theme of my effort.

What I mean by this word is not what first comes into our professional mind these days. Automation has attracted me as much as the next librarian. I am captivated by the computer. The printout catalog entered early into my library school teaching. I effected one of the first modulations from traditional reference to Information Science, at Florida State, as the cover of an issue of *American Documentation*, some years back, will attest.

My colleagues in Florida know the cross I bore in the forties and fifties convincing librarians there were no such things as "non-book" materials, and how I finally, I effected what some called a "shotgun marriage" of librarians and audiovisualists, with my book *Instructional Materials.*

Yes, I believe in computers, in telefacsimile, in video recorders, in 16mm projectors, in the overhead with its transparency overlays, in the tape recorder for oral history; in the whole repertoire of machines and electronics that will make us more efficient. I am not like the librarian who boasted, "It takes longer and costs more, but we are automated." I have passionately advocated taking advantage of every invention technology has blessed us with. But all of this is not what I mean by innovation.

What I mean by innovation welcomes improved hardware as a means to a new dimensional education. But hardware is not the crux of my kind of innovation. The innovation I have in mind is on the drawing board in about 100 experimental colleges. Mostly, these colleges are not the ones that head lists of outstanding institutions of higher education, that appear periodically, in such frequently cited media as the *New York Times*, or *Newsweek*, or even the education issue of the *Saturday Review*. They are not, necessarily, Harvard and Yale, and the Ivy League colleges; almost always followed by Chicago and California; and perhaps, more recently, including near the bottom, with apology, a few institutions from the South.

The innovating colleges I have in mind almost never make the academic counterparts of the Associated Press "Top Twenty" weekly football lists. For the innovation I have in mind, you would have to look at colleges like Antioch in Ohio; Florida Presbyterian; Kendall in Illinois; Monteith of Wayne, in Michigan; Oklahoma Christian; Stephens in Missouri; the University of California at Santa Cruz; Elmira of New York; and perhaps 100 or more experimenting senior colleges like them. But increasingly, I believe, we will watch the Junior College, that higher education phenomenon, the public version of which was born right here in Illinois, at Joliet, hardly a half century ago.

Why the junior college? Because it is remaking higher education in America. In this phenomenon is emerging a prototype for the college to come. Call it community college if you prefer. It makes no difference now, since U.S.O.E. has established the two terms as synonymous.[1] The Community College has dared to break with some sacred traditions of higher education.

The first affront is to *elitism*. Since this is Chicago, we are in hallowed country for the proposition that only 10% of the people are higher educable Not so far from here, the president of one of our state multiversities with some 40,000 enrollments was asked, recently, "How many students do you now have?" He replied, "Oh, about 10%." Clever as this may sound, it is nevertheless untrue. As far back at least as the 1948 Chicago Institute, I dissented with Dr. Faust's position that college is for the "chosen few."[2] In my naive philosophy of higher education, college is for every one. The Junior College has had the courage to open its doors to all high school graduates. It has, in effect, said to the *Elitists*: "Sissy; anybody can educate the top 10%, in your kind of education. Let's see you higher educate the dropout, and the rest of the 90% who might never get the chance to go to college."

I agree with the Junior College position. There is some support for the conclusion that violent revolution occurs in nations when the 10% higher educated can no longer communicate with the 90% not higher educated. Spearheaded by the Junior College, the United States is about to accomplish another first in world history. While many of the other countries do not even yet have universal elementary education; and most do not have 100% secondary education; we are about to provide college for every one.

By 1970, we are told, more freshmen will be entering junior college than any other type of higher educational institution. This is true in Florida now. To this point, Junior Colleges have tried very hard, at least in their college parrallel program, to comply with the Ivy League rules. To enable their graduates to transfer to senior colleges and universities, Junior Colleges have followed unquestioningly the prescriptions of tradition. But there are now some signs of dissent among the Junior College leaders. The thinking ones are unwilling to concede that the traditional colleges have a monopoly on liberal education, or on academic standards. Among some educational statesmen, there are a few who contend the elite colleges are the opposite of liberal. Among the Ivy League institutions, for instance, the authoritarian curriculum of predatory subjects and a rigid teaching method describe a dogmatism that repudiates liberalism. Judging by the campus unrest, there is something less than satisfaction with what the leaders of elitism have defined as higher education.

What we must recognize is that today's campus revolt is proletarian. It is a protest against academic elitism by the new student masses our American trend to universal higher education has created. The larger, than ever before, college population rejects the predatory curriculum which the academician flaunts as liberal. Students, overwhelmingly, are objecting to the lockstep of classroom-centered education. Young people, everywhere, resent the growing impersonality caused by numbers, and the faculty-administration persistence in enforcing the higher education folklore of the past, by introducing mob scene registrations in gymnasia, at the beginning of the term; and computerized evaluations at the end. This policing is far more brutal to them than any that has yet been used by municipalities to preserve peace in our streets.

No wonder our young people are looking increasingly to the community junior college. Like a breath of fresh air, these new institutions are reviving the true liberal education. Without abandoning the general education requirements that senior colleges and universities have made foundational for a bachelor's degree, the Junior College has liberalized the curriculum by introducing new areas for study. Not deterred by the conventional hierarchy of disciplines that places a Berlin wall between so-called liberal, and so-called *vocational* studies, the Junior College has contended that all knowledge has potential for living, as well as for making a living. And the history of education is on their side. Subjects high in today's curriculum were very low in the middle ages; and *vice versa.*

So I return to my opening sentence: if I were to come out of retirement to become an academic librarian again, I would experiment and innovate, not with library techniques and automation, but with library education. I would accept the challenge Chancellor Emeritus Harvie Branscomb hurled at us in *Teaching With Books,* back in 1940:[3]

> "To sum up, the fundamental need for the college library is to develop a distinctive program of its own . . . it has been too imitative of other institutions."

And I would seek my inspiration from the educational concept of Junior College, even if I happened to be librarian of a senior college or of a university. For the time has come to admit mutual reciprocity between the lower and upper undergraduate levels, without condescension, and with more than an outside chance that it has been the traditional institutions that have "watered down," and not been truly liberal.

And now let me explore library-centered educational innovation. Universal higher education means not only numbers, but the widest range of individual differences college has ever known before. It is therefore hopeless to continue lockstep education in the classroom. More than ever before we must move to independent study. Contrary to the previous honors program assumption, independent study, properly conceived, prepared for, and guided is especially suited for the wider range of talents now found in our student population. Furthermore, individual independent study provides, as Winslow Hatch has indicated in his thoughtful little

"New Dimension" booklet a real measure of quality education.[4] The first concomitant of a distinctive library-centered higher education, therefore, is a learning mode that is carrel-oriented, rather than classroom controlled.

The second element is a teaching mode that is predominantly concerned with matching individual differences in students with individual differences in Media. For the first time in the history of education there are now so many media, in a variety of formats, a range of levels, and an assortment of subjects that the individual differences Binet and Simon told us about a half century ago exist in humans can be found in the proliferation of media pouring out all over the world today. It is, therefore, hopeless to continue a type of classroom centered, group teaching that was necessary when media were few and expensive, and when the range of individual differences was far narrower than now. Indeed, the phenomenon our orators like to refer to as "explosions"—of population and of knowledge—dictate abandoning the horse and buggy method of education we have known in the past, and to take up a new learning mode—an educational program that is, in Dr. Branscomb's words, "the library's distinctive own."

In 1934, at Chicago's world fair A.L.A. convention, I read a paper in which I predicted the coming of this new educational dimension in the colleges and schools.[5] My colleagues have been good enough to credit the beginning of the current Library-College movement to that paper. But I acknowledge the origin of the idea in Thomas Carlyle's essay, "The Hero as Man of Letters," in his book *Heroes and Hero Worship*. From this essay comes the frequently quoted commencement line:

"The true university is a collection of books."

But what is not so frequently quoted is the context. Carlyle's contention, as far back as the middle of the last century when books were not as plentiful as now, was there is little the professor can do for the students beyond teaching them to read. The rest the students must do for themselves, largely independently. This is the heart of the Library-College concept.

When a college is a library and a library is a college it is a Library-College. Fundamentally, the Library College reverses the present relation between classroom and library. Instead of meeting classes at regular hours and working in the library irregularly, when time permits, the Library-College student is more likely to set for himself a regular schedule at his exclusive work-bench, his very own library carrel, a carrel, which thanks to the technology which I applaud, is becoming "wet" with dial access to a variety of media. In this learning design the student speaks less of attending classes and more about reading.

There is a precedent for this in England, where there are a few colleges that might even make our top twenty with the Ivy League. During my Fulbright year in the United Kingdom I heard students and tutors constantly using such expressions as he is *reading* in physics; he is *reading* in economics; he is *reading* in philosophy; rather than that he was attending classes in those subjects.

Now, by reading, the Library-College means more than just reading in a hard cover book; or even a paper back, serial, or other form of print. The Library-College means reading in what I call "The Generic Book," in my editorial for the *Saturday Review* during the observance of the first National Library Week. Any medium of communication between man and his environment; between man and man; and between man and God is part of the Generic Book. Under this definition, a 16mm film is a book; so is a magnetic tape; or a transparency overlay. Discs and dioramas; maps and microtexts; community resources and computer assisted instruction are varying formats of the generic book. You can understand, perhaps, as my students have all of these years, why the term "non-book materials" causes a hayfever-like intellectual allergy in me. Philosophically, I have described the Generic Book as the sum total of man's communication possibilities. If I may push theory a little more in this pragmatic profession and world of ours, I speculated in the *Saturday Review,* as I have elsewhere in my writings, that communicability is the only real evidence of life, just as the French General in World War I had insisted that death is incommunicability.

I am not alone in this position that reading is related to all the means of communication. In a thoughtful little book, published by Columbia University, titled *What Is Reading?* Frank G. Jennings wrote:

> "reading . . . is not restricted to the printed page. Actually, it never was . . . throughout his history man has "read many things: the flight of birds, the guts of sheep, sun spots, liver spots, and the life lines on the hand. He

has read the lore of the jungle, the spoor of the beast, and the portents in a dish of tea . . ."[6]

In all the furor and exhibitionism over Marshall McLuhan there is really only one fundamental truth: the format of a medium may affect communicability. Our individual differences are such that some of us may understand a subject better by viewing it on television; or hearing it on tape; or taking a field trip; or concentrating on a printed page. Learning is enhanced by the choice not only of the right subject, and the right level of maturity, but by the choice of the physical makeup of the medium.

Forgive this philosophical transgression. It is a preface to an understanding of the library's own, distinctive educational program. I believe we are on the verge of realizing it in some 100 experimental colleges. I believe that any campus where independent study is the learning mode not only for a select few, the so-called honors group, but for all of the students, an element of the Library-College is emerging. There are evidences that the liberalizing influence of the junior college through its extension of higher educational opportunities to all is spurring individual, independent study to universal acceptance as the new learning mode.

As a concomitant to this learning mode innovation, I see ahead some startling revolutions in academic librarianship. Considering the standard elements of stock, staff, facility, and services the impact of the Junior College mass higher education phenomenon can cause major professional innovations in college and university libraries. To meet the wider range in the individual differences of our student population, we will have to reorient book selection to media selection. That this has not yet been done is illustrated by the two new, fine junior college book lists that have appeared this year.

STOCK-MEDIA SELECTION

Dr. Frank Bertalan has compiled a *Junior College Library Collection*[7] of over 17,500 titles that is clearly curriculum related. He has maintained the high standard of selection that made his previous list the guide for so many beginning junior colleges. I daresay the new list will be just as helpful. But as it stands now it is a list of print books. There is a promise of other media format lists to come.

Similarly, Dr. Helen Wheeler has restricted her *"Basic Book Collection for the Community College Library*[8] to "the first five thousand book-titles," that is, print books. Although Dr. Wheeler advocates the concept of the Materials Center, which we originated and pioneered in Florida, right after World War II, she accepts the boundary line we have drawn, professionally, between print and so-called audio-visual aids. Her appreciation of these latter formats, however, underestimates them educationally less than Marshall McLuhan underestimates print.

But selection aids of the future, I dare to predict, in the light of educational innovation, will erase the artificial boundary between so-called print and audiovisual formats. To illustrate the unity of media, and therefore of library materials, I cite the fact that both audiovisual and library professional literature claim at least these common formats: maps and globes; pictures (although the audiovisualist likes to use the term flat picture); museum objects, which the audiovisualist sometimes calls *Realia*; exhibits, bulletin boards and displays. Recall that the Carnegie Corporation donated a million dollars to libraries as early as 1928, to develop phone-record collections. This was some time before the audiovisual movement renamed these formats *discs*. Librarians have been in the vanguard of oral history production and preservation, which rely heavily on the magnetic tape. And what will you say to the librarian-encyclopedia editor who crossed an audiovisual transparency overlay with a printed book. If the cross-media approach of which we have made so much of late, means anything at all, it means unity among all of the media of communication, and therefore a library obligation to balance selection not only by subject and level, but by format, as well. I predict the next selection aids will be media aids, rather than print-only lists.

STAFF

More carefully defined levels of library practice, in the future, will at long last release the professional from semi-professional and clerical tasks for truly professional performance. Automation and even newer technological developments are helping, but even more promising is the growing recognition of the middle level paraprofessional, now officially renamed by the A.L.A. committee the Library Technical Assistant. The impact of the junior college on this innovation in personnel is evidenced by the fact that almost all of the education for this new career has occured in the two-year institutions. This month, *Tex-Tec* will be published,[9] which represents the first state-wide syllabus for the training of Library Technical Assistants. As libraries add paraprofessionals, as well as clericals, and take advantage of library technology, professional librarians will have released time to devote themselves to participation in the new learning mode of independent study, and assume full partnership in faculty research. Since the new type of Library-College education is dependent upon knowledge of media as well as of students, there is no faculty segment better prepared than the knowledgeable librarian. Just as the artificial line between print and audiovisual formats is being erased, so also is the separation of *faculty who center their instructional effort in the classroom* from *faculty who teach with media in the library*. Indeed, if the independent study trend continues, the time may soon come when the classroom instructor will have to fight for faculty status.

FACILITY

Library facility planning has already begun some spectacular innovation. As a countermeasure to the growing impersonalism on our multiversity campuses, which student revolters place at the top of their disaffections with American higher education, cluster college patterns are developing. Again, as a Fulbright Fellow to the United Kingdom, I have been taken with the British organizational plan. For example, Cambridge University has over 30 colleges, none of which has an enrollment of over 500, thus insuring faculty-student personal relations. The University of California at Santa Cruz, which will have an ultimate student population of 27,500, is organizing its campus into small colleges, each under 1,000. So also is the new Florida Technical University in Orlando. Michigan State has begun to organize colleges around individual dormitories. Here is a trend that will modify the classic site specification for the center of the campus, into several sites each central to a cluster college campus.

The carrel-centered, independent study, learning mode suggests we can no longer accept a standard that seats 25% of the student body at one time. Already we have colleges that seat half of their student body at one time. Oklahoma Christian has 110% seating, to insure an individual carrel for each student and provision for enrollment increase. Steadily, these carrels are becoming "wet," with dial access to a widening range of visual and audio media.

When it comes to stock accommodation, it is no longer adequate to plan for so many volumes of print, hard and soft cover, with a general allotment for something called an audio visual area. Now, definite provision for housing other media formats of the generic book, along with equipment necessary, is an integral part of total stock accommodation planning. Furthermore, something called a core, must be designed to handle dial access, possibly computer controlled.

But planning for staff accommodation will be most sensitive. The usual 100 square feet per full time staff member to accommodate workers in technical processes, reader services, and other conventional library functions, will have to be augmented by office, seminar, and classroom space for instruction. For, in the Library-College type of institution, the library becomes the main institutional building. And the faculty to be accommodated teach more in the library than they do in the classroom.

An example of library architecture innovating in this direction is Dallas Baptist College. In an approximately square building, a central core accommodates the generic book stock. Around that core are student carrels to accommodate at least half the student body. And utilizing the outside wall space are service areas and technical processes; instructional areas housing faculty offices, seminars, classrooms.

SERVICES

Which brings us to the critical services. With the professional librarian relieved of most of the organizational tasks of the past, he can for the first time assume the major responsibility for developing a distinctive library education program, such as Chancellor Branscomb challenged us to do. Curriculum-wise, we have two fundamental areas to contribute, areas we can hold our heads high about, because they are truly liberal and substantive. The first of these is what the prolific author *anon* heralds on many of our campus buildings as the "half of knowledge," that is knowing where to find it. And who better than we can teach the use of media. In the past we have admittedly accomplished less in teaching the use of the library than we had hoped for. But now, with independent study as the dominant learning mode the student is impelled by academic survival to understand media, to master the skills of information retrieval.

The other area I call, simply, *Knowledge*, a capstone synthesis of the separate predatory disciplines. Although we have now integrated at the general education level separate chemistry, physics, and geology courses into something called *phy sci*; botany, zoology, physiology into *Bi Sci*; sociology, political science, economics, and even history into *social sciences*; philosophy, art, literature, religion into *humanities*; a further integration of these three areas is called for; a bringing together of what C. P. Snow has called the "two cultures."

The librarian, as a natural generalist is best equipped, of all faculty, to accomplish this. Through his professional concern with epistemology, with the classification of knowledge, with the provision for a *generalia* class; with his traditional imparitality toward all of the disciplines, he can be trusted, more than his colleague specialists, to represent the universes in perspective. In addition, through his own learning device of browsing, he can encourage a cross-subject approach to an understanding of the riddles of the universe. He can, indeed, introduce into the bloodstream of the learning life that phenomenon which science has but recently discovered, namely, serendipity.

Yes, if I were to return to academic librarianship today, I would devote myself to educational innovation. Because I believe that is part of the high role I see in our profession of destiny. To those of us who celebrate the "grass roots," and always being practical, what I have said will sound like a dream. But to quote the South Pacific song, how can our dreams come true if we never dream.

I know that our campus tradition will interfere with realizing much of what I have suggested. That is why I look to the experimental rather than to the Ivy League colleges for a break through. Even more, I look to the junior colleges, who seem to have the courage to question all the folklore academicians have taken for granted. At any rate, whether we want to or not, campus revolts will force us to other less creative measures. Why not then experiment in newer directions? Why not experiment and innovate on our own.

I believe in this profession of ours. I have faith that what we know and are, will point the way to a higher education more liberal and substantive than anything the world has known before. My faith in our next professional generation of librarians convinces me we will yet develop a prototype for the higher education to come.

REFERENCES

1. U.S.O.E. *Library Statistics,* 1966-1967. G.P.O., 1967. p. 2.
2. Chicago University. *Preprofessional Education of Librarians.* 1949. p.109-14.
3. Branscomb, Harvie. *Teaching With Books.* 1940. p. 9.
4. Hatch, Winslow. New Dimensions in Higher Education. U.S.O.E.
5. Shores, Louis. *The Library Arts College. School and Society.* 1935.
6. Jennings, Frank. *What Is Reading?* Teachers College, Columbia University, 1965. p. 11.
7. Bertalan, F. J. The Junior College Library Collection. Newark, Bro-Dart Foundation, 1968.
8. Wheeler, Helen. *A Basic Book Collection for the Community Junior College.* Hamden, Conn., The Shoe String Press, 1968.
9. Shores, Louis, *et al. Tex-Tec.* Syllabi for the Education of Library Technical Assistants in the Junior Colleges of Texas. Washington. (Communication Service Corporation, 1967).

8.

THE LIBRARY JUNIOR COLLEGE

A New and Larger Role for the Library in the Junior College

(Article published in the *Junior College Journal,* 1966, 36:6-9)

THE PRESIDENT of one of our great multiversities with an enrollment of over 40,000 was recently asked, "How many students do you have?" He is reported as answering, "Oh, about 10 per cent."

For years, college catalogs have gloried in proclaiming to the educational world that only top students are wanted. That institutions of higher education have settled for less in no way denies overwhelming faculty preference for the superior student.

That is why I begin by taking my educational hat off to the junior college. In effect, the junior college is saying to the senior colleges and universities, "Sissies. Anyone can educate the superior 10 per cent. Let me see you do something with the other 90 per cent."

The junior college, has, in fact, undertaken to higher-educate all of the people. By 1970, we are told, there will be more freshmen and sophomores in the junior colleges than in all other types of higher educational institutions combined. The junior college will, in effect, be *the* agency for helping the United States realize the goal of being the first nation in the history of the world to provide a *higher* education for all of its people. Such an achievement may well mean that for the first time leaders and followers will be able to communicate with each other intelligently enough to forestall violent uprisings.

If the junior college is to succeed in its courageous undertaking, however, it is just possible a new higher educational concept will be required. Evidence that American higher education is undergoing a major revolution can be found in several trends. Representatives from ten experimenting colleges invited to Wakulla Springs, Florida, by Florida State University in the spring of 1964, to describe their experiments, revealed changes so far-reaching as to point toward a new American higher education.

First among the organizational trends in the experimenting colleges is an effort to remove the growing impersonality caused by mounting enrollments. This is being accomplished by organizing our multiversities into a number of small colleges somewhat after the pattern of the British university. Notable American examples in this category can be found at the new University of California at Santa Cruz, and at the older University of the Pacific.

Top among the educational trends is the increasing reliance on independent study in the library as the mode of learning. Whether the pattern is honors reading, or autonomous courses, or tutorial instruction, it is evident that the oral lecture and the classroom group contact are steadily being subordinated to library reading. The class contact, as a measure of education, and the complex paraphernalia of course credits are in some danger of being replaced by the more individualized type of learning encouraged by the library, or by its renamed successor, "the learning resource center."

Because the junior college has already established itself as the most flexible and receptive of all higher education institutions, and because its challenge and opportunity are unlimited, I expect these two major trends will find their fulfillment in these first two post-secondary years of schooling. The form this fulfillment will take presages something we call a "library college." Somewhere in these United States a junior college will follow these trends to their ultimate and present us with a true "library junior college." It is even possible that among the new junior colleges of Alabama or Florida one will undertake to experiment with the idea of a cluster of small colleges, one of which will be a library junior college.

With this in mind let me undertake to describe the role of the library in a junior college committed to capitalizing on the trend to independent, library study.

The role of a library in any college is to support the college's educational objectives. Traditionally, the library does that by acquiring the library materials needed to support classroom instruction, by organizing these materials for ready use, and by circulating them to faculty and students as needed. In addition, libraries provide an information service, called reference, which assists readers to locate materials and information.

In many colleges, orientation in library use is given during opening school week and later in course units planned as part of English and other courses. Some colleges offer a one-hour-a-week course. Recreational reading is encouraged through browsing room collections, bulletin board exhibits, reading lists, book reviews, and lectures.

Audiovisually-minded librarians who have of late operated with presidents in adopting a more spectacular name for their libraries, such as learning resource center, also procure, organize, and disseminate newer educational media. Let it be understood, as the head of the first professional library school to require audiovisual instruction, that I favor all of these media. But let me make it clear that some of these "media" or "carriers," as others choose to call them (a term which has a malaria connotation for me), have always been integral to the concept of a library.

Years before the audiovisual movement was born libraries had files of pictures. Although librarians did not call them "flats" they were the same kind of pictures. Three-dimentional ones, too, could be found in the old stereoscopic collections. Maps and globes, bulletin boards, exhibits and displays, museum objects (now dubbed with the fancy name of "realia" in the A-V literature) abounded in the up-to-date library. As early as 1928 the Carnegie Corporation gave a million dollars' worth of phonograph recordings (now called discs) to colleges. Many other formats like slides, transparencies, microforms, and even filmstrips and films are now found in school libraries. As programed materials and electronic devices appeared, automation-minded librarians leaped to adopt the equipment.

The procurement, organization, and distribution of all these different kinds of materials are inherent in the library function. They constitute what I consider the library's ancillary role in support of classroom inshtruction. But the nature of classroom instruction is undergoing a radical transition. Oral communication of facts, by the teacher is steadily being replaced by bibliographic guidance to a variety of sources. This stimulates the student's independent search for, and discovery of, facts and concepts at the pace indicated by his individual readiness. As independent study becomes ever the dominant mode of learning, the classroom teacher takes on more and more of the bibliographic competence of the librarian. In the process, the librarian assumes ever more instructional responsibility. As a result, in such progressive colleges as Stephens, Antioch, Florida Presbyterian, Mt. San Antonio, Parsons, and an increasing number of experimenting colleges, the line between classroom teacher and librarian has been nearly erased, and they are both now part of a faculty with a concept of a library college.

It is this kind of a library college that I hope the emerging community junior college will become. For this new library junior college I see a realization, at long last, of the true role of a library in a college. To paraphrase Thomas Carlyle, the true college is a collection of books; the true faculty is a group of teachers who can interpret this collection of books to students in such a way as to guide learning toward a liberal education which encompasses both living and making a living.

In the library college the library has its present ancillary function of procuring, organizing, and disseminating the collection of books. But, in the library college, the library also has an initiatory function as well. The library serves in a unique, instructional role. It is best qualified to teach that "half of knowledge which is knowing where to find it." And as for the other half, it is the only teaching unit in the college which can provide an unlimited interdisciplinary approach to knowledge.

LIBRARY COLLEGE ENROLLMENT

Community junior college enrollments now range from under 100 to over 10,000. The first organizational requirement is that the library junior college enrollment not exceed 1,000. This can be accomplished in even the largest, urban junior colleges by following the example of the English university and of the experimenting U.S. universities like that at Santa Cruz, California, of organizing the campus into a number of small colleges. Each of these colleges can be given an accent if desired. One can point toward the natural sciences; another toward the social sciences; a third toward the humanities; and still others toward various terminal vocational trainings, or even toward community adult education. This would mean, for example, instead of our Miami-Dade Junior College in Florida handling its 17,000 students across the board, it might create some seventeen colleges with not over 1,000 enrollment each.

In the recent survey of student opinion about American higher education no one criticism was more consistent than that directed against the growing impersonality caused by our multithousand enrollments. Reorganization of our very large institutions into smaller, manageable colleges would restore some of the intimacy that is inherent in a good learning environment.

The library college is, therefore, a small college with an enrollment of not over 1,000. This is a necessary prerequisite to the library organization which is to serve the library college.

Quantitatively, from 10,000 to 20,000 items of all format categories should put a library college library in business. This number range should meet the criticism directed at the present junior college library standards by presidents of very small junior colleges.

Qualitatively, basic items in all of the subject areas represented by the curriculum should be included. Proportions and exact titles will have to be based on such joint selections from existing library aids and subject bibliographies as subject specialists and librarian generalists agree. And, of course, these selections will have to be limited to funds available.

In addition to the subject areas, important general and intersubject materials must be included. Essential is a basic reference book collection. Perhaps no less than 10 percent of the total initial and subsequent annual budgets should be expanded on reference materials. Another 5 percent, at least, should be used for general periodicals and indexes. Besides subject, two other criteria enter into adequate, qualitative selection of library materials. One is level of sophistication. To meet individual differences, content and form difficulty should range from tenth to sixteenth grade. The other is format. I have developed a classification of format in my book *Intructional Materials*. This describes five major classes of print, several of graphics, projections, transmissions, community resources, and electronics-mechanics.

Specifically, such audiovisual materials as films, filmstrips, slides, transparencies, microforms are part of a modern library collection. This means that the projectors, readers, and other equipment necessary for the use of the materials must be housed and maintained in the library. Similarly, discs, tapes, radio and television sets, along with players and recorders, belong in the library. The whole range of materials grouped under the heading of graphics requires not only the materials but the facilities for producing them.

THE LIBRARY FACILITY

One segment of the collection that must not be overlooked in the community college library is local history. An archival collection of letters, documents, pictures, and memorabilia pertaining to the localities, counties, cities, neighborhoods, campus, and library should be assidously sought out, gathered, and organized from the start. Its psychological as well as scholarly significance cannot be overestimated. Such are the dimensions of an adequate collection of library materials for the library junior college library.

To house this junior college library, several variations on the principles architects and librarians have developed over the years may be called for.

Site specifications in the past have always said "central" for the library. This remains true. But for the large institution that turns to the recommended cluster of small colleges, multiple centers will have to be established, one for each college.

Stock accommodation recently has been influenced by modular construction, which presented floor reinforcement throughout the building on the assumption that a bookstack load may be shifted. It is here suggested that a fixed stack location of the bulk of the stock might have certain advantages of economy and still provide considerable modular space for reader and staff accommodation. It is almost necessary in view of the greater range and variation of formats in the modern library. Fixed stack areas for storing films, discs, tapes, microforms, bound journals and newspapers, and infrequently consulted hard cover print suggest advantages.

Reader accommodation recommendations in the past have ranged from 15 per cent to 25 per cent of the total student body to be seated in the library. In view of the independent study mode in the library college a seat for every student is proposed. Instead of tables with chairs for from six to twelve students, individual carrels are advocated. Such an arrangement is not less economical in space. In the reading rooms of its library, Mt. San Antonio Junior College in California has demonstrated that it can seat just as many students in carrels, efficiently arranged, as it can at tables. And what is more important, Mt. SAC has established that better concentration is achieved in a carrel atmosphere than in a group-table study climate.

There is not space here to examine all of the elements that go into the planning of an adequate library facility. In the past few years I have consulted with junior college presidents, their librarians and architects, on most of the new library building planned or constructed for Florida junior colleges. Rather than enumerate the pitfalls and innovations, I would like to cite some considerations for the advanced type of library required by our library college.

Since reading is the principle library activity, too much attention cannot be paid to lighting. Ever increasingly, viewing and listening have become important to learning. Therefore, acoustics and darkening are essential considerations, especially in areas designated for preview and pre-aud. So are an adequate number of outlets for projectors, recorders, playbacks, computers, and other electronic equipment. Even the quiet reading room providing listening posts with headsets that permit the reader to hear what he is studying without disturbing those about him.

Air-conditioning is now almost universally planned for library facilities. Its importance in the preservation of expensive materials is only less than its contribution to human effort.

Floors previously tiled with rubber or linoleum, are now being carpeted. This is a welcome reform that has proved fully as economical as hard covering and much more conducive to creative study. In addition to compact carrels for students, more generous-sized ones should be provided for faculty, to perform double duty as study and office. One junior college library has planned a seminar conference room for every four such faculty-carrel-offices. Call this type library a learning resource center and it will convey a concept more active than the passive role too often associated with the traditional library; or if it will obtain more funds. But the truth is, the good library has always been a significant learning resource.

LIBRARY ORGANIZATION

At the top of the library college library reorganization are the two influences of cooperation and automation. The trend to central processing is now so marked that we have working examples of statewide central acquisition and central preparation for public and school libraries. Why not for junior college libraries? At the moment, Dr. Jahoda, chairman of the information science area in our library school is working with the libraries of the Florida public junior colleges on a feasibility study of central processing and co-operative information retrieval. I have reviewed the findings of his first survey which were shared with presidents and librarians of the junior colleges at a Florida meeting.

The purpose of central processing is to free the librarian from technical routines that can be accomplished more economically, centrally. Since book discounts are based on volume of business, central ordering for all of the junior colleges promises a considerable saving at that point alone. By utilizing the computer printout, instead of the printed or manually prepared catalog card, it is estimated that book catalogs in quantity can be produced centrally for the holdings of all the junior colleges individually and collectively. Furthermore, the fantastically speedy computer can keep all of these book catalogs continuously up-to-date and reveal the location of scarce and expensive materials for loan and reproduction.

You can see that automation for acquisition and cataloging appeals to me. Its capabilities for circulation have also been demonstrated. I believe in enlisting machines and electronics wherever they will help free the librarian for the high role of instruction that has often been denied by the press of housekeeping duties. But I caution against the overuse of automation. I have seen too many examples of high school principals and college presidents who employ automation for advertising purposes solely. In one such instance, the librarian, after triumphantly displaying a computerized charging system, wryly admitted it costs more and takes longer than the old way, but it surely impressed the visitors!

As in all libraries, ancillary services must not suffer because of innovation. Faculty book selection must be more speedily implemented by procurement and processing than before. Circulation of reserve and nonreserve must proceed as long as there is a demand for these kinds of loan. Photoprocessing of excerpts must be made simpler and less costly. There is no need to detail the advice that the old services must go on, lest the new be condemned for interfering.

But an immediate start can be made with the new, merely by accenting some of the older, minimized services. For example, information science makes much of something called "profiles of interest" of their researchers. This is really not much more than some of us have done for our faculty when we noted their investigations in progress and called attention to new publications in their areas of interest. Some of us have done something like that for instruction as well.

THE LIBRARY JUNIOR COLLEGE

Experimenting colleges in the United States are steadily replacing group teaching in the classroom with independent study in the library. That is not to say that the classroom is disappearing. What is happening is that the relationship of classroom to library is being reversed. Oral instruction by the teacher is giving way to guided individual reading. In the changing mode of learning, librarian and classroom teacher together have introduced a more personalized learning process, one that takes into account the individual differences of a wider range of students than ever before in the history of higher education.

This changing educational pattern confronts both the junior college and its library with a new challenge and an extraordinary opportunity. Because the junior college has proved it is less restrained by the forms of the past, I believe it will create a new dimension in higher education, one that is equal to the task of educating all of the people. It will achieve this dimension by utilizing a new learning resource library as never before.

The library junior college idea deserves a try. If it helps this nation achieve its educational goal it may mean that for the first time in history the followers will be literate enough to understand and work with their leaders.

9.

THE RESOURCES OF LEARNING

(Address delivered on the occasion of the ground-breaking ceremony for the Learning Resource Center, Edison Junior College, Fort Myers, Florida, January 31, 1967.)

PRESIDENT ROBINSON, Faculty Colleagues, Ladies and Gentlemen:

On this significant occasion I bring you greetings from your State University in Tallahassee. We are proud of Edison Junior College; of our distinguished alumnus who is your president; of the College's three supporting counties—Charlotte, Collier, Lee. From my experience as dean and professor at Florida State University for the past 21 years, I can assure you that no better students, or finer young men and women have come to our University from any of the other of Florida's 67 counties. I salute you this momentous day, and express my humble gratitude for the opportunity to share in the joy of this event.

My message for this occasion is devoted to three significances. Perhaps you should be as grateful that there are only three, as a Yale audience was once at commencement when the speaker limited himself to only four. On that occasion, the speaker devoted himself to the four letters that spelled Yale. For a half hour, each, he expressed himself on the significance of Youth, Ability, Love, Efficiency. At the end of the two-hour address, the weary audience heard the chairman comment, "Thank God, this is not the Massachusetts Institute of Technology."

My first significance is the *community junior college movement*, generally, in our nation, and particularly, in our state. Others have already defined, and redefined, adequately this higher educational phenomenon. Statistically, its significance will be attested in the United States by 1970, when far more freshmen will be enrolled in junior colleges than in the senior colleges and universities combined. That fact has already occurred in Florida public higher education. You must know that our 25 public junior colleges in this state currently enroll 81% of all the beginning college students in tax supported institutions of higher education.

In my opinion, this is as it should be. For too long, the senior colleges and universities of the nation have made a fetish of admitting only so-called "superior students," meaning students gifted in certain curriculum, predatory, subjects, who scored high on specified measuring instruments. Only the junior college has had the courage to say we also want students who are superior in other areas of human existence. For, the junior college has recognized the fact that all of the people are gifted in different ways, and that a society can be good and great only if education commits itself to a philosophy so simply and eloquently expressed as the opening sentence of the current Edison Junior College Catalogue:

> "The purpose of Edison Junior College is the fulfillment of the individual." (1966-1967, p.9)

This educational philosophy has been especially well encouraged by our Florida Division of Community Junior Colleges, under the creative leadership of Dr. James L. Wattenbarger, Assistant State Superintendent of Public Instruction. No tribute was ever more deserved than that accorded him by the Florida Association of Junior Colleges in convention at Daytona Beach, last November, as a recognition of his ten years of dedication.

My second significance is that of Edison Junior College, for this community of three counties. As a member of the Tallahassee Chamber of Commerce, and of the Tallahassee Lions Club, these many years, I have boasted many times, in many places about the excellence of my city, my county, my state, and my nation. Not so long ago I did this on a 42,000-mile circumnavigation of the world, in places as far away as Cape Town South Africa; Hobart, Tasmania; Manila, Philippines; Tokyo, Japan; to say nothing of the 14th time in Paris; the 4th time in London; the third time in Rome and the second time in Frankfort. Indeed, those who know me say my deanship is only a front for my real boast—the fighting Seminole football team of Florida State University.

As an experienced booster, therefore, I cannot imagine beginning and ending my boasts about this community of Charlotte, Collier and Lee Counties with anything else than Edison Junior College. You must know what you have in it. If education is steadily becoming our greatest industry, as almost all industry as well as government now acknowledges, then you have made one of the most profitable investments in America. And your managers, the president and his faculty, have given you one of the great successes in a nation known for its superlatives.

Think of it. Edison opened its doors September 1962. By the time of the fifth school year opening, you have 1,226 students enrolled. The quality of the education offered these students receives the commendation of the critical state survey board. And this results in full state accreditation, a recognition, I assure you, highly coveted. It results also in full accreditation by the stiff, regional accrediting agency—the Southern Association—a recognition which other junior colleges, some of them in this state, have not attained in twice that time. Indeed, as you know, one of our public school systems is now desperately trying to regain accreditation from the Southern Association. If this achievement by Edison Junior College does not top the list of prides published by your local Chamber of Commerce, and by your Lions Clubs, then I am not the seasoned booster I'm supposed to be. I venture to predict that Edison already has influenced and increasingly will influence the desirable individuals and industries we seek to attract to Florida, and induce them to locate in the counties of Charlotte, Collier and Lee.

My third significance relates to this new building for Edison Junior College, the ground for which we are breaking this forenoon. *Learning Resource Center* as a new name for a library has come into vogue recently because it communicates better the changing role of this essential educational unit. There are, of course, those practical-minded citizens who contend it is harder to get money for a library than it is for something with a more glamorour identification. I have a very good, but defensive friend, who is a member of a board of education, very conscious of his own limited schooling, but who should not be. He said to me the other day, "why don't you educators talk less about libraries, and more about learning resource centers, like the one at "X" junior college. It's teriffic. Instead of dry, dusty books I can't even read, there are all kinds of gadgets, like computers, and automatic charging machines, and electronic push-button machinery, with red, blue and green lights going on and off all over the place, like in those "double 07" movies. You can get my money for that any time."

Whether that reaction is representative, or not, of those who control the money strings, I don's know. But the fact is that our modern libraries are much different from what they were. They are different in the kind of materials they contain, and in the role they now play in the education of our young people. Let me try to explain quickly, because I want you to share with me the excitement ahead for Edison students and Faculty when this new Learning Resources Center will be ready for use.

First of all, a book no longer means only a hard cover with pages of print in between. For a long time, now, the book has meant many other kinds of materials, or what we technically refer to as *formats*. Format is defined as the physical makeup of a book. Before the invention of printing, about 1450, the word *book* meant a hand-written manuscript, usually on parchment. And, before that the word *book* meant a roll; and before that a clay tablet, with cuneiform writing. After the 15th century, the hard-cover book was supplemented by other formats: the map; the newspaper; the magazine. Soon, paperbacks, and then charts, broadsides, pictures, cartoons, comics began to be included in the composite term *book*.

Toward the end of the last century, libraries, increasingly, combined with museums to include all kinds of things: rocks, butterflies, models, objects of many sorts. These, too, became a part of the generic term *book,* which can be defined as all the records of civilization through which man communicates. And then began the series of inventions which resulted in the phonograph record, the tape recorder, radio, and other sound media; the motion picture, filmstrip, slide, transparency, and other projections, all of which we sometimes designate as *audio visual* materials. Most recently a series of electronic media have appeared, aided by the spectacular computer, reinforcing programmed learning, and the teaching machines. All of these, too, are part of the generic book. I have identified and classified over a hundred different formats found in our schools, and colleges, and libraries, in my book, *Instructional Materials.*

Because of this range and variety of materials the modern library has taken on a different profile. Many of the new formats of the generic book require special equipment and maintenance for their use. Motion pictures require projectors and screens, for example; tapes and discs need recorders and playbacks. All of these media and their equipment have changed the architecture of the traditional library. To project certain visuals, the attention formerly paid to lighting for reading must now be complemented with consideration for darkening. The former *quiet* associated with libraries must now be surrounded with a new accoustical treatment to permit the sound of radio, television, and other media.

But if the physical changes caused in the library by the newer media, and their equipment, have dramatically converted our libraries into learning resource centers, the educational innovations have even more spectacularly revolutionized learning. Some 75 colleges and universities in the United States, labelled "experimental," are steadily developing the trend toward independent study by the student into something new called the *Library-College. A Library-College* is a colleges that is entirely a library, or a learning resource center. In the Library-College the student learns at his own individual pace, under the bibliographic guidance of the faculty. Instead of receiving oral, group, instruction in a classroom by an instructor, he explores and digs for himself at his own private work bench in the library, called a *carrel.* The modern, so-called "wet" carrel has dial access to a variety of the formats that constitute the generic book. For example, if he wants to hear a tape, or a disc of the foreign language he is studying, or of a symphony he needs to know for his course in music appreciation; or wants to hear John Gielgud speak Hamlet's soliloquy while reading Shakespeare's play; all he has to do is dial for it, and it comes to him in his carrel. A filmstrip, a slide, a motion picture, a transparency, a tv kinescope, all may be at his finger tips to reinforce his individual study efforts. Or if he missed a lecture, or wants it repeated, it is probably canned in the library collection available for transmission to him.

Spectacular as this learning appears, much of it is already in operation at colleges like Oklahoma Christian, Stephens, and even our own Miami-Dade Junior College. Its educational soundness is reinforced by our American commitment to universal higher education. As more and more of our young people go to college, the range of individual differences steadily widens. It becomes ever more difficult to teach in the classroom by the old oral methods. In the middle ages, when books were scarce, before the range and variety of educational media could match the individual differences in pupils, classroom teaching was necessary. Today, such an educational procedure is becoming steadily more frustrating to students and teachers alike.

Everywhere there is evidence of a new generation of students, and a new breed of teachers. Faculty are using the library in teaching more than ever before in the history of education. As you watch the better teachers work with their students these days, you admire their creative efforts in matching media with the individual differences of their students. The result is an education that is tailored to the individual aptitudes of your child.

This is the wave of the future in the new college education. It is this wave which this new learning resource center heralds. By our ceremony here today, Edison Junior College informs Florida that here in Fort Myers the foundation is beginning, not only for another college building, but for a new kind of education. With this ground-breaking for the new Learning Resource Center, another community junior college in Florida's developing higher educational network serves notice it is ready to prepare the next generation for the society of tomorrow.

I congratulate you, the people of this community, the faculty and students of Edison Junior College. I predict great things ahead for you, for Florida, and for our Nation. May God bless your combined effort.

10.

IF I WERE PRESIDENT
(Of a Junior College in Minnesota)

(An essay for the Minnesota Junior Colleges Faculty Association, Minneapolis, April 26, 1968. For *Library-College Journal* publication.)

INNOVATION WOULD be the theme of my administration.

If I had not before, I should most certainly now, take up B. Lamar Johnson's challenge to experiment.[1] I would go even further. Out in what is sometimes called left field I would try, boldly, a new kind of learning, a new design for the first two years of higher education. And I choose that dfescription for the junior college deliberately, over what is commonly included in the definition, "post-secondary school education," because I believe the needed new dimension for higher education in America will come, not from the Ivy-league, nor even from the other four-year colleges. I believe the prototype for the college of tomorrow will come from the Junior College.

I believe this because the Junior College has shown that basic courage which is fundamental for the demands of our times. Too many colleges pride themselves on catalog statements that declare "we accept only the superior student." Of course, some colleges that still need enrollment look the other way when cash-paying parents compensate for drop-out youngsters. But there are still the colleges that brag about stiff admissions. These admissions are based on high grades in the predatory subjects, the so-called "disciplines" that have a monopoly on the liberal arts label. Not so the Junior College. It has had the courage to say to the rest of American higher education, "Sissy. Anybody can educate that kind of student in your kind of education. Let's see you salvage the drop out. We challenge you to take any high school graduate, discover his talents and develop them to the utmost in the interest of the individual and our society." The Junior College has accepted this challenge.

Having accepted this challenge, the Junior College, or the Community College, since U.S.O.E. now equates these two terms as synonymous,[2] must now also accept Dr. Johnson's dare to experiment and innovate. The essential reason is in the acceptance of the first challenge to higher educate everyone. Whether we like it or not, the United States will soon be the first nation in the history of the world to have universal higher education.

I happen to like it. As far back as 1948, at least, I dissented with one of Robert Maynard Hutchins' leading disciples, Dr. Clarence Faust, at a University of Chicago Institute over the higher education philosophy of "elitism."[3] I believe in College for All. Call it the "College Phobia" if you will. I am prepared to debate this educationally or philosophically. I do not agree with the cleverness of the President of one of our state universities with an enrollment of about 40,000 students, who, when asked the other day, "how many students do you have," replied, "Oh, about 10%." God gifted all of us, my simple and naive faith tells me. I defy research to prove otherwise. It is part of the college's responsibility to discover the individual talents its admitted high school graduates have, and to strive with its students for their self realizations.

One reason why I believe in college for all is based on the lessons of history. A good case can be made for tracing the decline and fall of nations, in significant part, at least to the assumption that 90% of the people are not higher educable. There is evidence that violent revolutions results when the higher educated 10% can no longer communicate with the 90% who are not higher educated.

But College for All presents more problems than college for 10%. For one thing, numbers generate the impersonality in higher education that, by latest poll, is indicated to be the number one cause of current campus revolts. For another thing, universal higher education introduces into the classroom the widest range of individual differences ever found in college before.

As for numbers, one of the most promising solutions is the experimenting with so-called cluster college campuses. As a Fulbright Fellow to the United Kingdom, I came under the influence, early, of the British university organization pattern. No matter how large a university grows over there, personal relations between faculty and students is protected by seeing that no college on the campus has more that 500 students. A number of our universities have begun to imitate this organizational pattern. One of the notable examples is the University of California at Santa Cruz. I want to see the Junior College, as its enrollments mount, organize its campus into smaller units. Indeed, I believe it would be advantageous to innovation and experimentation if, as a Junior College approaches 1,000 students, it would activate a second unit, or college, on its campus, instead of permitting a mob scene to develop each registration day in its gymnasium.

One of these colleges might well be experimental. I would like to see one of these a so-called, now, LIBRARY-COLLEGE. When a college is a library and a library is a college, it is a Library-College. There is no one concept of a Library-College, as you will gather by reading the book published by Drexel Press in late 1966.[4] But there are certain fundamental philosophical and educational concepts in the idea of a Library-College.

Since some have been kind to trace the origin of the movement to my address before the 1934 Chicago World's Fair convention of the American Library Association.[5] I want to repeat my acknowledgement to Thomas Carlyle, the English 19th century essayist. In his famous book, *Heroes and Hero Worship*, he has an essay enentitled "The Hero as Man of Letters." There occurs the line quoted so often by commencement orators:

"*The true university is a collection of books.*" To this should be added what else Carlyle says. Essentially, he maintained that higher education is the ability to read, and that is all the professor can do for the student.

But reading does not mean in the Library-College concept that all education comes out of a hard cover book. Remember, writes Frank G. Jennings in his thoughtful Teachers College Columbia book, *This Is Reading*:[6]

> ". . . reading . . . is not restricted to the printed page. Actually it never was . . . throughout his history man has "read" many things: the flight of birds, the guts of sheep, sun spots, liver spots, and the life lines on the hand. He has read the lore of the jungle, the spoor of the beast and the portents in a dish of tea . . ."

What Frank Jennings is suggesting is that there is something I have called the "generic Book." This comprises all the media of communication, between man and his environment, between man and man, yes, even between God and man. This was the thesis I tried to espouse in my editorial for the *Saturday Review* on the occasion of the observance of the first National Library Week. This is my purpose in my book *Instructional Materials*, where I accomplished what some have jokingly referred to as the "shotgun marriage" of librarians and audio-visualists. I believe this is the most important thing Marshall McLuhan is trying to say in his much publicized *Understanding Media*.

In terms of the Library-College, a fundamental aspect is the concept of reading and of the library. Call it "Learning Resource Center," or Media Center, or Instructional Materials Center, or Materials Center, or any other fancy name you can think up for the old fashioned label; it is still basically a library. And before you try to convince me otherwise, look back at the literature and see how long ago my writings introduced the Materials Center concept.

Educationally, these are some of the important principles in the concept of the Learning Resources Center, and the generic book. Books have appeared in a great many formats since the beginning of history. We use format to mean the physical makeup of a medium. A clay tablet; a papyrus manuscript; a page printed from movable type; a celluloid film, filmstrip or transparency; a stereo disc or a magnetic tape; a community resource; a teaching machine, if any are still around; or a remote console of a computer. These are only a few format illustrations of the generic book. Unless we, as college faculty, have this concept of the book, we don't understand the Library-College idea.

Books have also appeared on a great many subjects. Two knowledge classifications currently used to arrange media in libraries—the Dewey Decimal and the Library of Congress system—illustrate, epistemologically, what man knows, and has communicated through media. These library classifications also relate the predatory disciplines of our curriculum with so-called co-curricular subjects, as well as with each other. Every college faculty should look at these and other library classification systems from time to time, to restore perspective, to engage in interdisciplinary exploration, and who knows, to join the growing cult of serendipity.

And books are also appearing in a wider range of levels. The significant educational principles here are that it can now be said that individual differences in students can be matched with individual differences in media. Which means that all of our frustrations (since a couple of Frenchmen named Binet and Simon made us aware) caused by the fact that learners' inherited talents, plus their environmental influences, are as individual as the lines on the palms of our hands, may be relieved.

Relieved how? Relieved by a new breed of faculty. Relieved by Junior College professors who will at long last take up the challenge delivered by Chancellor emeritus Harvie Branscomb in his classic study for the Carnegie Corporation back in 1940. He titled his book, *Teaching With Books.* In a sense, he found the college faculties of the United States almost allergic to books. Overwhelmingly, he seemed to indicate that our college teachers simply don't know their books of all formats, subjects, and levels, well enough to match them to the individual differences of students. In 1968, nearly three decades later, it is probably true that many of us still do not have an adequate knowledge of the generic book.

We are not entirely to blame. Because we are the children of a generation which had fewer learning resources, and therefore could not teach with books. Furthermore, we are products of a higher education in which the generic book *per se* was subordinated to subject, to psychology of learning, to curriculum development, and to a host of other things. If we were ever taught anything about the generic book itself, it was taught incidentally, and with vindictive insistence that this was educationally right.

But on the bright side, there have always been faculty members whose preeminent method was based on teaching with books. Librarians have always referred to them as "library-conscious." I know social sciences colleagues who have been bibliographically more expert than librarians. But what is more important, they have aroused the individual talents of students by matching media to personal aptitudes in a way that would make any non-housekeeping librarian drool. I have admired science teachers like Professor Postlethwaite at Purdue who has marshalled a variety of media formats to innovate with his audio-tutorial method. And who has not known literature instructors who have reinforced the visual reading of Shakespeare's *Macbeth* with an audial reading by John Gielgud, concurrently, at the library's listening post.

These examples herald the new breed faculty of the Library-

College. They presage the shifting of the learning locus from the group climate of the classroom to individual study of the library carrel. The Library-College does not eliminate the classroom. Rather, the classroom is reoriented to the trend toward independent study, and to the phenomenon of many and varied media. This reorientation accepts Winslow Hatch's measure of quality education as the student's ability to study independently.

After the inspiration from Carlyle's famous essay, the next most stimulating experience along the Library-College way came from a 1928 visit to the campus of Antioch College in Yellow Springs, Ohio. I recall observing the opening, September class in beginning Economics. The late, great labor arbitrator, Dr. William Leiserson was the professor. He spent the class period overviewing the subject, indicating some major issues of economics publications. A selected reading list, a few pertinent facts, some suggested subjects for investigation, his office number and hours, were most of the things I remember on the stencil he handed to students. And then those words: the next time this class meets you will ask for a meeting. Until that time, happy reading, thoughtful writing on the four papers you will hand in, and as many conferences with me and your fellow students as you feel a need for. Oh yes, I plan to deliver about six lectures on my specialties, dealing with things not yet in print. You are invited as well as every other Antioch student who wants to come.

This was one of my earliest experiences with what we now call independent study, or honors reading. Antioch called theirs autonomous courses. Various other names have been given by other colleges: tutorial at Harvard; preceptorial at Princeton. But the Library-College independent study mode differs most with the honors reading concept. The Library-College does not believe this method should be reserved for the superior. On the contrary, the Library-College believes independent study may be most advantageous for those students the elite college would not consider gifted. In any case, the Library-College favors the learning mode that is carrel-centered independent study, supplemented by classroom, laboratory, field trip and other experiences.

In this learning mode, the faculty member can perform creatively, both in instruction, and in his own research. Performing as the good physician, the teacher studies his student profiles, and matches media for the particular learning situations. Skillfully he chooses format, level, subject as the student confrontation suggests.

There is still a significant place for the textbook format, as an organizer, as a review medium, as a tool with more potential than we as teachers have yet realized. But there is also a much underestimated learning format on the open shelves of our libraries in the basic reference books, that remain so largely undisturbed. Because we have never been properly introduced to the good encyclopedia, there as so many among us who fear it. Our fears are based on improper student use, caused largely by teacher ineptness with encyclopedia authority, scope, arrangement, treatment, illustration. I daresay there are many more than the few colleagues I know who have not yet discovered the transparency overlays, that were first introduced about a decade or more ago. If we know transparencies at all, they have to be in connection with the overhead projector. And there are still too many teachers who haven't begun to use them that way, either.

I discovered the encyclopedia's potential for an A grade as a senior in high school. Forgive me for the material motivation of a grade. This is not unknown even among today's students. But you will probably have to forgive even more for the greater motivation. It came from the teacher I was to have in Economics. She was one of my earliest "crushes." Although at least ten years older than my seventeen, she was so beautiful to me that I was positive that we were destined for each other. I knew I had to make an "A" in her class.

Accidentally, I decided to read the article on Economics in the *Encyclopedia Britannica*. It helped. I read another encyclopedia. It helped even more. Unaware of what I had done, I had accomplished an overview of the whole semester's content. I had built up anticipation. I began comparing the teacher's scope and sequences of the subject with what I had come to expect from my pre-school opening encyclopedia reading. When she did the expected, I reinforced her presentations from my readings. When she departed, I challenged inwardly most of the time, but audibly on occasions when I could no longer keep quiet. Both the teacher and my classmates began to look to me for confirmation. I clinched my "A" early. But I must report to you, not because of my encyclopedia reading, that before the semester was over my romance was transferred to a coed nearer my own age.

And then there was the Botany professor, my colleague and

next door neighbor who never used another format vital to his subject. The evidence was in the fact that he had not once previewed or borrowed one of the several time-lapse motion pictures in our library. If one would like to see how a budding plant blossomed out into an array of multisplendored petals, it is not always convenient to hang around for several days to watch the process. But time-lapse photography can store and retrieve the whole phenomenon for you, and communicate the spectacular effect in whatever time you can spare. How to get to my neighbor, Max the botanist, to show this to his students, is not a simple problem. College professors are human too. None of us likes to have our ignorance exposed.

So I used the old librarian technique with faculty colleagues. "Max," I said, in our living room, "I need your help. I've been asked to review a new film. It happens to be in your field. I barely passed in college botany. I don't know a thing about the subject. Will you review it for me, and save me some embarrassment?"

Max viewed the film. What I expected happened. "What do you call that technique?" he asked. "Time-lapse." He said, "Where has that been? I could use that a million times a month. Send me all of them." "But Max," I reminded, "the purpose of this showing was to help *me* out."

Well, there are at least a hundred different media. Florida high schools exchange with high schools in the Latin American country of Colombia. A foreign language teacher, if he stood on his head, could not communicate the nuances of the spoken language to his students the way teenagers, even in different countries, can to each other. As a biology teacher, you can get as many anti-vivisectionists in your community against you as possible, and it is doubtful if you will communicate more about the anatomy of a frog than that transparency overlay in the encyclopedia, meticulously prepared by a team of scientists, photographers, artists, and offset printers. Do you know that everytime that encyclopedia goes to press, that set of transparencies costs the publisher $70,000? Oh yes, some of us can assume condescension toward these other formats, but we owe them a trial, at least.

The significance of all these media, their different formats, levels and subjects, is that without them independent study as a learning mode is much less. Without them, the Library-College is handicapped. For in the Library-College the library is in fact, not in oration, the learning center. It is so because the Library-College library stocks a range of media formats, levels, subjects to match the individual differences of the campus community. Increasingly, the Library-College library provides dial access to all of these media, at the student's individual workbench, now known as a "wet" carrel because of its electronic equipment. It provides this also for faculty offices, now located in the library, to the concern of some of the more conventional librarians. And there are even seminars, classrooms, laboratories, auditoriums, in several newer library learning resource centers.

Which brings us to the students. Before someone else says it, let this paper record it: they are first. We have our share of demagoguery, too, at educational conventions. How many times have we heard a bit of innovation aborted by the platitudinous remark, "But the students come first." I have never doubted that the students come first with all of us who teach. Where we differ is on the way to put the student first.

I happen to believe that the Library-College is more student-centered than any other learning pattern we now have. It begins with the student's individual differences. It attempts to determine this through a student's interest profile that is based not only on his course program of the term, but on his co-curricular interests, his occupational objectives, his avocational pursuits, his mental and spiritual development, and a host of other considerations. Furthermore, it invites faculty-student dialogue on his curriculum, on his learning mode.

The Library-College creates conducive working conditions. Where the conventional college provides as high as 25% library seating for the student body at conventional tables, the Library-College insists on an individual carrel for each student. Oklahoma Christian College, for example, has 10% more carrels than there are students enrolled. This does not mean regimentation. If a girl insists she can study better in her domitory suite when her three roommater are discussing shifts and boy friends, let her try it. And if a boy wants to work on his calculus while roomies tackle and guard are practicing blocking in their room, okay. But at least every student knows he has a private workbench he can retreat to any hour of the day, and increasingly of the night.

The new breed Library-College student will be as varied in his interests, and aptitudes as are the media in their subjects and levels.

If there is a hint of regimentation in Library-College learning, compare it with what many have called the classroom lockstep. Essentially, the independent study learning mode evolves over the four years from outer to inner discipline. Rights match responsibilities, so the student's study habits increase his independence.

If I were president of a Junior College, new or old, I would experiment in several directions. One of them would be organizational. I'd move toward the cluster concept, with at least a second unit or college on campus, from the start. One of the very first experimental units would be a Library-College. Evaluation of both the students and college would be undertaken with traditional measures, at least during the transition. Once the Library-College proved itself, new and better measures might be introduced.

As we look at the nearly 100 experimental colleges in the United States today, many of the features of the Library-College can be discovered. At least one four-year college has committed itself to the idea. But I believe a Junior College will be the first to achieve acceptable success as a Library-College. I believe this because of my faith in the courage and creativity of the faculties of our Junior colleges. With anticipation I look forward to the emergence of the Library-Junior College.

REFERENCES

1. Johnson, S. L. "Education and the Junior College." *Junior College Journal.* 1967.
2. U.S.O.E. *Library Statistics, 1966-1967.* G.P.O. 1967. p. 2.
3. Chicago University. *Preprofessional Education of Librarians.* 1949. p. 109-14.
4. *The Library College*: ed. by Louis Shores, *et al.* Drexel Press, 1966.
5. "The Library Arts College." *School and Society.*
6. Jennings, F. G. *This Is Reading!* Teachers College, Columbia University, 1965. p. 11.

11.

IF I WERE PRESIDENT
(*Of a Junior College in Florida*)

(An essay for the Florida Junior College Faculty Association, Daytona Beach, November, 1966.)

IF I WERE President of a Junior College, innovation would be the order of the day.

I would encourage experiment by every faculty member as a component of his daily effort. Despite the hazard and the loss from trying untried ways I would consider the investment of time and thought necessary to continuing improvement. If industry can afford to invest in effort that has no immediate, or even ultimate payoff, then surely education which has prided itself on research can do no less. In short I would take up B. Lamar Johnson's challenge to the junior colleges to experiment more,[1] and make this papa of junior college innovation proud of the younger generation.

My experimental encouragement would point in two directions, mostly, although there would be no intention to turn off explorations in any area of college education that could stand a little bit of fresh thinking. But the two areas that would attract me most, as a junior college president, would be institutional organization and student learning, in reverse order.

INSTITUTIONAL ORGANIZATION

I would begin my organizational thinking with a prejudice that stems from my Fulbright year in the United Kingdom. I believe in the intimate education of a small college. And I believe such intimacy can be preserved no matter how large a college grows. And junior colleges will grow ever larger; never doubt that. The president who says to me, we have only 300 students now, and we probably will never have more than twice that number is shutting his eyes to the phenomenon of our nation's commitment. The United States is the first nation in the history of the world to undertake universal *higher* education. And mind you, this is being undertaken while most of the world's peoples do not yet profit from compulsory elementary education, and secondary education is still a luxury reserved for the economically elite. With that sort of a commitment on the part of our country, it is unrealistic for any college president, and especially any junior college president, to expect permanently small enrollment. My guess is that any junior college that prospers will have over 1,000 students by 1970. And as soon as a junior college approaches that enrollment, impersonality begins to elbow its way into the learning climate.

So if I were President, one of the first bits of innovation would aim at forestalling the mob scenes in college gymnasia on registration day. I see no virtue in exposing students to long-line waits for enrollment in courses that counsellors have advised. Indeed, my experimental thinking would tend toward eliminating the class course itself, and replacing it with a better learning mode. But of this later. Now, my presidential thinking would take a cue from the British university. I would aim to reorganize my junior college into a cluster of units or colleges, not shying away from the terminology *Junior University* as the designation for my institution.

The Junior University organization can be compared to our solar system, with the university as the sun and the colleges, whether on one or several campuses, the planets. Each college might be limited to about 400 students, and hopefully a minimum of 20 faculty, perhaps eventually as many as 40 when our national commitment to education advances above even our present acceleration.

Educational facilities for each planet college would include, basically, the library. It may be called a materials center, a learning resources or an instructional resources center, or any one of the other names we have recently adopted. Most of you know that the Florida State University Library School, of which I am dean, led the nation in the concept of unity of materials, was the first professional school for librarians to require audio-visual competence for all of its graduates. You know also that we have one of the few nationally recognized departments of information science and that we are heavily commited to computerized information retrieval as well as to computer assisted instruction. Consequently I am sure you will give me credit for awareness if I use library and learning resource center synonymously.

At this point, let me finish consideration of the organizational innovation I suggest. In addition to the library which is the college in my concept, it is possible that each college will have dormitory for resident students, food and recreation facilities; but no classroom or laboratory building, no gymnasium nor infirmary, and no administration building, unless the college campus is at some distance from the university campus. The shape of the college building may resemble the Oxford or Cambridge college pattern—quadrangular about a green common, or it may take a distinctive Florida architectural design. Only, the college must provide an opportunity for intimate academic life.

The college faculty should be headed by a dean of Instruction and Resources. In his dual role as college librarian and dean of faculty he will be in a strategic position to help the library-college idea work. There is a precedent for this combined position in the deanship B. Lamar Johnson held at Stephens; that Stafford North holds now at Oklahoma Christian. And I daresay there are variations on this pattern in a dozen or more experimenting colleges.

Probably during transition, present major subject areas should continue to have department heads with the necessary number of instructors and other ranks. The Library-College will be able to begin with a fairly bibliographically competent nucleus of its faculty including some librarians who are more committed to instruction of students than to management of materials and equipment. Much of the housekeeping now done by librarians and classroom teachers will be performed by adequate clerical staff and increasing centralized automation of technical processes.

Facilities that serve all of the colleges and do not require duplication will be centrally placed in the university. These will include administration building, infirmary, and gymnasium. The university campus will include also an auditorium, supplementary lecture halls, and classrooms. It *may* include a chapel, if Congress will relax the Supreme Court's rigidity on this question. But the University campus *will* have the largest library, or learning resource center, including major equipment like the computer, and other expensive hardware, as well as research and rare materials. Here the requests for materials and equipment from the colleges will be received, procured, prepared, and distributed. With this organizational innovation overview of the Junior University we proceed to a consideration of the prototype junior college.

A planet Junior College in a solar Junior University will typically have about 400 students, 200 boys and girls. Heterogeneity will be accented by the ever widening range of individual differences concomitant with the trend to universal higher education. Interests and talents will be more diversified than ever before in the history of post-secondary schools. This will force all colleges and universities with the courage to admit the other 90% to reexamine the folklore of pedagogy as never before.

Basic to this reexamination will be a review of the class contact as a measure of education. It is now accepted without challenge, almost, by U. S. colleges that the number 120 or its conversion from semester to quarter or annual credits equals a liberal education. To move on to graduate work all one has to do is to present a transcript which records like a bank book the necessary credit. Convenient as this is for our registrars, counsellors and deans it is perfectly mystifying to the universities of the United Kingdom and to higher educational institutions in other countries. Abroad they cannot understand our measures of education in terms of the number of class periods attended. And if we truly want to meet the challenge of universal higher education we will question the classroom as the locus of learning.

Over the centuries through the middle ages group instruction in classes was both possible and a necessity. The possibility occurred because of the restriction of higher education to the so-called "upper 10%" and the narrower range of individual differences intellectually among the educands. The necessity was caused by the limited number of books or media in all formats. This made it necessary for the professor to digest in class lectures the knowledge he had obtained from media to which he alone had access.

With the invention of printing and the repeated revolt of the masses, educational opportunity steadily extended to more of the 90%. But the educational habits of colleges and universities persisted. Despite the ever widening range of individual differences in the student population, teachers persisted in a group-class lockstep that based the lesson plan on a mythical average. Although printing first, and audio-visual production later, proliferated media, the school's greatest concession was to provide the individual pupil, free, an adopted single textbook. More progressive teachers developed with librarians something called reserve readings. But conservative classroom teachers persisted in their devotion to the single text. Not too many years ago, a history teacher in a Tennessee high school, in response to an inquiry for our Southern Association visiting evaluation committee about her use of the library said, "This year I think we will be able to finish the textbook by the end of May. Then I plan to send the class into the library as a reward to read anything they wan to." Fortunately, most of our faculty today, I hope, use the library heavily in their teaching and in their own preparation. But the locus of college learning is still the classroom. Indeed there are plenty of colleges who determine faculty status today solely on the basis of whether an educator teaches in the classroom.

This is not true however in an increasing number of experimenting colleges. At the Wakulla Springs, Florida Colloquium sponsored by Florida State University in 1964, ten universities and colleges engaged in experimenting reported on their innovations. Although these included such organizational patterns as the cluster colleges at the University of California, Santa Cruz and the University of the Pacific at Stockton; the dormitory-colleges at Michigan State; and such variations on the independent study theme as the Antioch autonomous course; the Florida-Presbyterian interterm replacement of class attendance by library reading; the favored areas of innovation were, unquestionably, in *organization* for the prevention of impersonality, in learning mode for the better recognition of individual differences in our growing student population.

THE LIBRARY-COLLEGE IDEA

In these innovations I see an inevitable trend toward what some of us call the Library-College. A Library-College can be described as a college in which the basic educational facility is the library, where students study independently under faculty bibliographic guidance at the individual student's aptitude and pace. The relation of library to classroom is almost inverse to present ratios of time and sequence. Instead of attending class regularly and reading in the library irregularly, the Library-College seeks to encourage regular work habits in the learning resources center and to provide seminar, class and group meetings as the student feels a need to augment his independent efforts. The origin of the Library-College idea is in Thomas Carlyle's essay "The Hero as Man of Letters" in which he made the often quoted assertion "The true university is a collection of books." In context he amplified,

The most the professor can do for the student is to teach him how to READ.

Educationally, the Library-College proposes to match individual differences in students with individual differences in media. There is now the widest range ever of instructional materials available. No longer are these limited either by subject or level of difficulty. What is more, these instructional materials come in a greater variety of formats than most of us identify, or at least relate properly. As early as 1935 I offered at Peabody in my library school there, probably the first audio-visual course in the South. Convinced that the film, the disc, the tape, the transparency, *et al*, stood educationally today in the same relationship to the hard cover book, as Gutenberg's first printed book stood in the 15th century to the vellum manuscript, and before that to the clay tablet, I began my lone missionary efforts to unify librarians and audiovisualists in our common effort to get teachers to know and use the treasures of these educational media in their educational effort.

It wasn't easy. You can go back in the literature to right after World War II when FSU Library School began its instructional materials mission with teachers, librarians, audiovisualists, administrators. You can read my debate with Ole Larsen, that brilliant audio-visual leader, in *Educational Screen*,[5] or my discussions in library journals; or the forum I conducted with the school superintendents of San Francisco and Grosse Point, Michigan in the *N.E.A. Journal*.[6] Or you can read my basic article on this concept in our own *F.E.A. Journal*.[7] The gospel was not easy to preach. Audio-visualists pointed their finger at me as a librarian; librarians accused me of being an audio-visualist renegade. In the end we did accomplish, as some one said, a shotgun marriage between audiovisualists and librarians, which resulted in our unique state certification in Instructional Materials, which about 12 states now imitate.

In 1960, my book *Instructional Materials* was published. It categorizes the various formats found in our nation's school and college libraries and learning resource centers.[8] Together these constitute what I call the generic book. It is necessary to see this classification of learning resources to understand what is meant by the content of the basic educational facility of a Library-College.

Our good junior college libraries in Florida have mostly begun by selecting and acquiring a basic collection of learning resources. To facilitate the creation of "instant libraries" for our new junior colleges, Dr. James L. Wattenbarger, Director of the Florida Division of Community Junior Colleges contracted with the FSU Library School in 1960 to develop basic lists of instructional materials.[9] Five of the eight lists were published and distributed without charge to Florida junior colleges by the division.[10] With the announcement that two national lists for junior colleges were in preparation the Florida series was discontinued. But the lists, now out of print, are almost continuously in demand, not only in Florida, but all over the United States.

The first prerequisite for a Library Junior College innovation is the stocking of the library, or the learning resource center, or any other fancy name you wish to call this essential facility, with a collection of media that will adequately match the range of individual differences of our student population. This stocking should be undertaken systematically by your faculty, and I include your librarian in the faculty, provided you employ that kind of librarian, rather than a glorified housekeeper.

The third prerequisite is a shift of the learning locus from the classroom to the library. Let me illustrate by describing the opening day in a beginning economics class I visited at Antioch one September morning quite a few years back. The instructor presented an overview of the subject such as you will find in a good encyclopedia. He followed this by distributing a self-study outline of economics, an annotated list of basic books, periodical articles, pamphlets, government publications, graphic materials, filmstrips, films, discs, tapes, and a few other media formats, which he had found helpful to an understanding of economics. On another stencil sheet was a calendar of commitments which included three papers on assigned subjects due about two weeks apart, and a term project to be selected by the student in consultation with the instructor. A mid-term and a final examination were also on the schedule. Office hours for student conference were indicated. The instructor concluded: "Happy reading, listening, viewing, writing, and conferring. The next time this class meets you will call for it."

Possibly the high I.Q. will favor this learning mode. But there is increasing evidence that individualized independent study is especially made to order for the less gifted student. Dean Richardson of the St. Louis Community College has observed aptly it is not so much our responsibility to teach the student as "it is the responsibility of the student to learn. This concept is particularly important when dealing with the disadvantaged student who, in many instances, seeks scapegoats for poor achievement."[11] Antioch began this year an independent study program for all of its freshmen which will presumably continue through the four years.

The fourth prerequisite for the Library-College is a facility planned for the independent study learning mode. A key component is the individual work bench for each student, exclusively assigned to him. I am well aware of the fact that the standards call for far less than that. Indeed I have complimented some of you for planning new libraries that would seat as many as half of your student body at one time. Good as that is for the present classroom centered instruction, it would totally defeat the Library-College concept. Basic to the independent-study, learning mode, is the requirement that each student shall have his own individual work bench where he can lock up his belongings, and come to work any hour of the day, or even night. This does not preclude his working in his room, if he prefers, or additionally; or in the lounge with the tv going, or interrupted by his date. But the individual work bench suggests a life situation which every young man and woman will have to face up to sooner or later: a place to report to for work. It, besides, insures at least one place for uninterrupted concentration, for meditation, an underestimated aspect these days of the go-go generation, for the inner struggle which is a necessary prelude to real learning.

Before this proposal is dismissed on grounds of economy, consider the dimensions of the basic carrel in comparison with present reading room table space in the library, and armchair or laboratory seating in the classroom. At Mt. San Antonio Junior College in California both carrels and tables were provided. It is the opinion of librarians that much more concentration occurs in carrel locations, and that if they had the building to do over, there would be a very much higher percentage of carrel than table space. To confirm which, they have steadily added to their tables the type of dividers indicated, to create individual stations. No additional space is needed.

At Oklahoma Christian College, where they have provided an individual carrel for each of their 700 students, they have studied the amount of time spent at these carrels each day. The average is steadily increasing as the faculty moves toward the Library-College concept of independent study. At present, it is about four hours a day. To meet the contention that it is uneconomical for these carrels to be unoccupied so many hours a day it is only fair to compare the number of unoccupied chairs in classrooms during a school day of hours comparable to library opening. But above that must be weighed our expanding educational commitment; our conviction that learning which is individually tailored is best; our growing contention that one measure of quality in education is the degree to which students can and do study independently.[12]

Overviewing the library facility for a planet college of 400 students, one design might call for a circular, or octagonal building, of which there are now examples. The center would be the stack for housing instructional materials of all formats, levels, and subjects. Around the stacks, 100 basic carrel/units, each unit providing four individual work benches, and such as illustrated in Exhibit B would be set. The outer, window circle might house 20 to 40 faculty offices, interspaced with five to ten similar rooms, perhaps two larger classrooms, and one assembly-lecture hall. The student carrels could be equipped with dial access to media of various degrees of sophistication in format, level, and subject. Depending upon resources and leadning mode, remote console for computer response is also a possibility, as well as facsimile for print media.

Inevitably, the question about laboratory arises. The answer may be in Purdue's audio-tutorial biology, which, as I understand it is "organized around a different approach to the laboratory experience. Instead of the traditional biology laboratory . . . the audio-tutorial laboratory consists of a series of individual stations, each equipped with a listening, and in some cases, a viewing device, and certain study materials. Individually, each student completes a series of laboratory experiences at his own rate. As he completes each sequence, he takes an oral examination to determine whether or not he has satisfactorily learned the concept that the experiments are designed to demonstrate."[13] Do you now see the basic carrel's flexible potential?

The fifth prerequisite is a curriculum which will complement the sacred subject specialisms with two general areas. High over the arch of our former library's doorway the words of that prolific writer *Anon* are still legible: "The half of knowledge is knowing where to find it." That half of knowledge is still sadly neglected, and woefully underestimated in our American education, from nursery through graduate school. At best it appears as a separate, required, although often unattractively offered, one-semester hour course in library use; at worst, as an incidental unit in our teacher education agencies, subordinated to every subject, method, or administrative course available to teachers. Obviously, if independent study is to have meaning, students must be equipped with a knowledge of media, *per se,* and not incidentally, in a way still found nowhere today. Perhaps the closest approach to this curriculum provision is provided at Monteith where faculty concede the experiment has given students a greater library sophistication than ever before. So the content of the first of two general areas study media, with heavy accent on the basic reference sources.

The second of these areas I would title "Knowledge." All of us made a big step away from specialism when we replaced separate beginning courses in chemistry, physics, geology with an integrated "phy sci"; in sociology, political science, economics, with social studies; in literature, art, religion, philosophy, with humanities. Now we need to take the next step: capstone science, social studies, humanities with an interrelated approach to the riddle of the universe. I am convinced that "In the beginning God created the heavens and the earth" not as a chemist from nine to ten every Monday, Wednesday and Friday, and as an economist every Tuesday and Thursday from two to four, and as a philosopher at three other hours during that week. Rather, I believe there is a unity to His universe that our curriculum sometimes strives to keep from our young people.

So I would propose that somewhere in our course of study we provide an opportunity for our students to cut across the boundary lines, not only of our sacred predatory subject specialisms, but of our newer integrated areas. Furthermore, I want this opportunity to provide for an experience which science, at long last has borrowed from science fiction, namely, serendipity. Who knows what discoveries our young minds will make in those interstices that fall between our curriculum studies. And the ready-made opportunity exists in an experience created by librarianship called browsing. Only I want our curriculum to recognize this unbounded area, to permit unrestricted student exploration, speculation, and meditation.

Well there you have it. I began this essay with a plea for innovation. I close this paper with a challenge to one Florida junior college to innovate by activating an experimental Library-College. A senior college, Jamestown in North Dakota, plans to do just that. I believe a junior college can beat them to the gun. The Library-Junior College can be set up on any junior college campus as a parallel to the conventional colleges. Instruments for comparison can be agreed upon in advance. The experimental Library-Junior College will differ in organization, facilities, and learning mode, fundamentally. Its faculty will be chosen for its degree of library sophistication and commitment to the independent study approach to learning. There will be no difference in the heterogeneity of the student body.

Some of you shared with me the Innovation conference at Magnolia, Massachusetts, last May. You know that experimentation is involving more of higher education daily. But there is considerable support for B. Lamar Johnson's original concern with the lack of experimenting junior colleges, despite the current *Junior College Journal* innovation issue.[14]

Because I believe in Florida and its creative community junior college movement, I have faith that one of us will try something very much like the Library-Junior College idea.

At any rate, if I were president, I believe I should encourage all innovations along the way.

REFERENCES

1. Johnson, B. L. "Needed: Experimental Junior Colleges," *Junior College Journal*. 1965. 36:2:17-20.
2. Stickler, W. H. *Experimental Colleges*; their role in American higher education. Tallahassee, FSU, 1964. 185 p.
3. Shores, Louis, *et al. The Library-College*. Philadelphia, Drexel Institute, 1966. 250 p.; "The Library Junior College." *Junior College Journal*. 1966. 36:6:6.
4. Carlyle, Thomas. "The Hero as Intellectual." (In *Heroes and Hero Worship*.)
5. *Educational Screen*. 1955. 34:112.
6. *N.E.A. Journal*. 1958. 47:343.
7. *F.E.A. Journal*. 1954. 32:112.

8. Shores, Louis. Instructional Materials. 1960.
9. Shores, Louis and Reed, Sarah. "Basic Materials for Florida Junior College Libraries." *Junior College Journal.* 1960. 31:98.
10. Basic Materials for Florida Junior College Libraries. Florida State Department of Education. 1960.
11. Richardson, R. C. Centralizing Library Services for the Multi-Campus Community College. (In Administration of Library Instructional Services in the Community College; Wayne State University, 1965. p. 10.)
12. Hatch, Winston. New Dimensions in Higher Education. U.S.O.E. 1965.
13. Richardson. *op. cit.*
14. *Junior College Journal.* 1966. Innovation Issue.

12.

THE MEDIUM JUNIOR COLLEGE

(Essay for the Fourth Annual Conference of Junior College Libraries in 22 states, held at Southern Illinois University, Carbondale, March 27, 1969. Although fantasy, this paper, like the other one in Illinois, was received with a touching standing ovation.)

TONIGHT IS March 27. But I ask you to imagine that the year is *1999*.

Few of us remember the Fourth Annual Conference held thirty years ago. But all of us know how fantastic have been the happenings of these past three decades.

In 1969 our United States seemed determined to prove the historical cycle theories of Spengler and Toynbee. By all the signs of the sixties we were repeating the course of the rise and fall of great nations in the past. It seemed inevitable that we would provide documentation for another Gibbon.

As you recall, there were two major party lines in 1969. The traditionalists were referred to as the Establishment. They were held responsible for poverty and prejudice at home; war in Southeast Asia. Washington was its headquarters, and the President of the United States its leader.

Opposing them were the Marchers and the Picketers. History now identifies them as the Demonstration. They opposed war abroad but increasingly stirred violence at home. They discovered problems, but considered solutions not their responsibility.

Pessimism permeated both the Establishment and the Demonstration. What was wrong with something excited them much more than what was right. They outdid each other denouncing President

Lyndon B. Johnson. In the very year when the Demonstration was supporting the Russian demand that the United Nations get out of the United States, the Establishment was displaying bumper signs on their automobiles that read "Get the United States out of the United Nations."

Not only our politics, but our culture, as well, was supposed to be dual. Indeed, one of the most frequently quoted essays in the sophisticated circles of 1969 was the English scientist C. P. Snow's *Two Cultures*. He contended there was a science culture and a humanist culture; and that the scientists knew more about the humanities that the humanists knew about the sciences. A few disagreed.

As we look back, science and its method appears to have had a near-monopoly on man's thinking. Not only was research the only answer for the physical, biological, and social sciences, but no history could be written about it. Even more shocking, in perspective, was the complete abdication of art to science. Novelists like Truman Capote boasted of their research. Realism became basic in fiction, drama and even poetry. Precise sensory descriptions of physical processes became the ultimate of the artist's effort.

So it was that during one Broadway season, 21 successive plays were praised by dramatists for their courage in exposing deviations. Theatres were packed by the oh-so-liberated to view perversions, addictions, abnormalities in human behavior. For example, a play with the brief title, "You Know I Can't Hear What You Are Saying when the Water Is Running" has a profound opening scene in which the hero is to appear stark naked, slowly approaching the audience on stage. This is to provide something super arty called "the shock of recognition." The play ran to packed theatre for well over a year.

Another darling of the Broadway stage included a bit of adolescent adultery between two faculty couples on a college campus with an irrelevant title "Who's Afraid of Virginia Wolf," and if you didn't see the relevance you were ostracized from the intellectual groups of both the Establishment and the Demonstration. Indeed, relevance in a title in those days counted heavily against the author. There was a gloomy play in those days staged over and over again by amateur groups with a title so senseless that even I am uncertain of the word sequence, and the one that makes the most sense is "The Hot Cat on the Tin Roof." If theatre in the latter days of Greece and Rome was an index of decline the United States certainly had its counterparts in the 1960's.

Nor was the fiction less indicative of a society's permissive decay. An adolescent classic with the title "Catcher in the Rye" could more critically have been retitled "Pitcher in the Corn." Its unheroic theme applauded more enthusiastically by adults than by teen agers, about whom it was written, once received this curt comment from a young adult library patron:

Librarian: You should read this book.

Y. A.: Why?

Librarian: Don't you want to know what goes on in a private school?

Y. A.: No. I'm having too much fun in Public School 88.

And on the adult fiction scene, one critic offered the readers six cliff-hanging seductions in what he considered the greatest novel of the century. Without four-letter words a novel was considered dishonest by the sophisticates; almost unpublishable by publishers in the gold rush. Eighteenth century writers who lived in squalid attic rooms and ate one meal a day had it easy compared to the mid-20th century novelist who had to wait three months for his fourth Cadillac because the manufacturer did not have it in the precise pink color; or the realist who felt restrained to spend no more than $20,000 on his cocktail party.

As we now study the videotapes of 1969 television entertainment we must temper our contempt for the appreciations of the older generation. Remember, they, too, considered the generation that preceded them hypocritical, dishonest, and unfair. You can find repeated without limit the platitude "Your generation has inherited problems you did not create," as if this was true of no other young generation in the history of the world. There is, however, no suggestion that the Hippie generation guarantees to hand a problemless world to the next generation.

It is easy for us to be critical of both the Establishment and the Demonstration, from our perspective. But we must remember that this nation had experienced the two most devastating world wars of all times; social and technological revolutions unprecedented in the record of civilization. What we must ponder is the overwhelming pessimism and realism that accompanied war and revolution. The question we must ask is why did neither the Establishment nor the Demonstration have the courage of optimism and romanticism? What made every one so pragmatic? Why did they glory in such cliches as the grass roots, and keeping your feet on the ground? Could they not, with their demonstrations for freedom see that a word they loved so much, like groovy, suggested a rut? How could they all, leaders and followers, repeat *ad nauseam,* their smug references to the two "explosions" of population and information; and the two gaps of generation and credibility? Was there no one to point out relatively how overestimated these gaps and explosions were?

No doubt about it, 1969 was one of the very low points in the history of the United States. Our national collapse seemed inevitable. Violence ruled our cities. Abroad it was considered smart to take money from America and call Americans ugly. But even worse was the defeatism at home. Our college campuses which should have been the centers of intellectual effort became circuses of exhibitionism. In the name of intellectual freedom a minority occupied academic buildings, interfered with the rights of those who chose to go to classes and shouted down speakers who disagreed with them. But out of this very campus chaos came the first revival of the creative optimism that had made this nation unique in the history of peoples.

There had been an old Establishment tradition that higher education was for the elite. Right here in Illinois there had been a leader of the theory of elitism, Robert Haynard Hutchins, for many years head of the University of Chicago. But also here in Illinois, at Joilet in 1962, the public junior college movement was born. From the start it pledged its faith to universal higher education. Whereas universities and four-year liberal arts colleges self-righteously proclaimed their restrictions to "superior" students, meaning those who could make high grades in predatory disciplines, the junior college boldly announced an open door policy. By 1970 there were more high school graduates enrolled as freshmen in junior colleges than in all other kinds of higher educational institutions. This was significant not only for education, but for society as a whole. Instead of marching, picketing, sit-downing, and exhibitioning physically against unjust discrimination, the Junior College courageously and intellectually demonstrated a solution, in which democracy functioned supremely.

That was only the beginning of a peaceful revolution with far reaching effects. Universal higher education introduced the widest range of individual differences in college population ever known before. The old learning mode of classroom lockstep and teacher lecture became impossible. Indeed, it was the persistence of this antiquated method of education which was basically responsible for student disaffection with the kind of college education they were getting. And so the Independent Study movement began.

At first this was reserved for the honors students, the elite who could be trusted to use their time properly. But college after college began to discover that independent study was even more advantageous to other students. Antioch College introduced its autonomous courses for all students. Florida Presbyterian College tried suspending all classes for a month in January with startling results. Emory University instituted Wonderful Wednesday. On the quarter system, all students had been required to take three five-hour courses, in which students attended classes every day for five days a week. In 1968 Emory tried suspending all classes one day a week—Wednesday—and the faculty and students took to it so enthusiastically, that it was extended. Oklahoma Christian, providing an exclusive work bench for each student, established the principles that faculty and students could agree on class meetings as infrequently as they deemed necessary.

But it remained for the Junior College boldly to revolutionize the learning mode. The Library-College idea had been advanced as early as 1934. The movement spread slowly at first, but picked up momentum beginning in the sixties. By 1970 it had an active organization—Library-College Associates, Inc.—with headquarters at the University of Oklahoma, and a quarterly journal, The Junior College picked up the idea and added new dimensions to it.

Junior College leaders understood well the reason for the classroom teaching mode of the past. Because media were available in limited quantities the teacher had to present information orally to groups of students in the form of lectures. As long as college was limited to the so-called upper 10%, the individual differences spread was not too wide and the lecturer could pitch his presentation on an average that did not miss too many of his students.

But as more and more students entered college the range of individual differences became so wide that an average presentation tended to bore the gifted and discourage the disadvantaged. Furthermore, by 1970 media of all formats, not only hard cover print, but paperbacks, graphics, projections, transmissions, and computer assisted media began to proliferate at such a pace that for the first time in the history of education individual differences in students could be matched by individual differences in media. Independent Study, individualized, emerged, increasingly, as the obvious learning mode.

There were many obstacles in 1970, however, to immediate replacement of classroom-centered teaching by carrel-centered learning. Most classroom teachers felt insecure in this new learning mode. Although they might feel they knew their subjects, and more shakily claim to know their students, they were unsophisticated in media. This was so, largely, because their teacher education insisted on teaching media very gingerly, and *incidentally*. Largely because of Junior College insistence, teacher education agencies began to introduce *per se* media instruction. Long before students were taught media in relation to subjects, or methods, or educational psychology, they were first being introduced to the whole range of media formats, from textbook to television, from magazine to motion picture.

But the old classroom teachers were not the only obstacles. Those who worked with media were divided. Librarians had a term which was always anathema to me, something they called "nonbook materials," but which they could never define, except by pointing to projectors or other equipment that they didn't want to maintain or operate. But you could put them on the spot when you asked them to identify as audiovisual such media formats as maps and globes, pictures, and even phonograph records. And Audiovisualists talked of print as something quite apart. It troubled them, however, when transparency overlays began to appear in hard cover books and the librarians began to take over microprojections like film and fiche, and micro opaques like 3 by 5 cards and 6 by 9 prints, and renamed projectors, readers.

Nor did this divisiveness end with the audiovisual-librarian schism. Soon the televisionists began to pull away from the audiovisualists and build their own empire. And then the computerized Information Scientists pulled away into their own organization. Nor did the separation stop there. CIA became a whole new empire when the exponents of computer assisted instruction decided their mission was more important than information retrieval. So it happened on some campuses that these two media groups separated expensively by purchasing two different and usually incompatible computers. On our campus for example, the information retrievalists switched to CDC, while the computer instructionists went to the IBM 360. All of this separatism bewildered educational administrators and classroom teachers. Where there were dual media centers, for example, a so-called library and a so-called audiovisual center, classroom teachers would be confident as to where to go only if the format was a 16mm film, or a hard cover book. When it came to a map or globe it could be in either place. If you wanted a picture you had to call it flat to get it in the A.V. center; and if you wanted museum objects you'd have to ask for them as realia in the A.V. center. When you ordered music for your classroom you specified phonorecords in the library; discs in the A.V. Center.

As early as 1946, Florida began to bring the Audiovisualists and librarians together. Out of their joint efforts emerged the first Materials Center, forerunner of the later Learning Resource Center. Florida became the first state in the union to establish a unified certification for all media personnel. It wasn't easy. Librarians and Audiovisualists continued to be wary of each other. But at long last most of them began to see that in unity there was strength. A tangible result was that the Legislature earmarked, one year, a million dollars to be used by the schools for Instructional Materials. Out of this came the first unified textbook, often referred to as the shotgun marriage of audiovisualists and librarians, my book, *Instructional Materials*. The 1969 joint standards of DAVI and AASL was the first official vindication by both groups.

Despite these obstacles the Junior Colleges spearheaded the new learning mode—independent study in individualized carrels supported by classroom meetings only when a group of students felt a need for coming together. As early as 1965, Oklahoma Christian College provided an individual carrel for each student. It was a radical step then, resisted by administrators as too expensive and uneconomical, although much more classroom space remained unused for longer periods of time. It was resisted by some educational psychologists who employed the now discredited questionnaire techniques of establishing that students didn't like carrels. And there was considerable reluctance in the ranks of classroom teachers and media personnel. But independent study overcame.

As we look at our media sophisticated Junior College faculties today we wonder how teachers and students tolerated their frustrations. Some very fine teaching is being accomplished by the subtle matching of individual differences in students with individual differences in media. But above all, students are learning with greater excitement through individual discovery. Instead of having predigested information fed to them by the lecturer, like pablum. They are acquiring many more facts much more rapidly by reading, viewing, listening, and even tasting, smelling, at their own dial access workbenches, the 1999 version of the student carrel.

Inevitably, this revolution in the learning mode converted the Junior College library into the modern Media Center. The most striking change appeared in the philosophy of evaluation and selection of media. Librarians had always practiced something called "book selection," which meant to them acquisition of hard cover print, primarily. Two of the last and finest aids in the Junior College field were published in 1968—one by Frank Bertalan; the other by Helen Wheeler. Both were quality bibliographic works. But they omitted what was then called "nonbook materials." This was especially handicapping to junior college librarians because audiovisualists were less bibliographically minded, and there were no selection aids for other formats comparable to those prepared by librarians for print.

Gradually, the unity concept for media began to take hold. In 1957 I had done an editorial for the *Saturday Review,* first projecting the concept of the Generic Book as the sum total of man's communication possibilities. Under this concept a film was as much a book as a hard cover collection of printed pages; or as the earlier formats of handwritten parchment manuscripts, or hand-chiselled cuneiform clay tablets. I had indeed quoted a fifteenth century monastery librarian who considered the manuscript format the only book; the new machine produced print "nonbook materials."

Up to 1970 book selection meant, primarily, selection by subject. I had tried to describe a three-prong approach to selection absolutely prerequisite to the changing learning mode of independent study. Almost as important as subject selection, I had insisted, were Level selection, and Format selection. Level had been easier to sell than Format selection. There was a ready made administration classification in what was then called K-6; 7-12; 13-14 for the Junior College level. Indeed, a few book selection aids like the

Children's Catalog had even offered a finer level discrimination in its grade by grade lists of books.

But the Format classification idea was hardest to sell, despite the celebrity exhibitionism of Marshall McLuhan. Perhaps this 55-year old man will be forgiven for his professional jealousy. Marshall McLuhan had served with him, briefly, on the ASCD Commission on Instructional Materials before he had attained celebrity stature. Despite all of the tv exhibitionism, the books that were printed top to bottom, sideways, and in imitation of Joyce's stream of consciousness, which industrialists financed lavishly for fear a competitor might be rated more uptodate. McLuhan stated one concept of extreme importance: the format of a medium may affect its communicability. My envy stems from the fact that I tore my heart out trying to communicate this point to my fellow librarians and audiovisualists in my writings and speakings. I simply did not communicate it in the rock and roll of that age, a beat that McLuhan captured groovily. His underestimation of print; his overemphasis on technology; his density on extrasensory perception have been exposed by our 1999 perspective.

Now we select media for our Junior College Media libraries from all three approaches: subject, level, format. But we are much more conscious of format now. We no longer make up lists of print format separately, and add audiovisual lists later, as they did back in 1969. We intercalate print, graphic, projection, transmission, resource, and computer materials, as some Florida materials centers began doing crudely in their card catalogs as far back as 1947.

This approach to media evaluation and selection has resulted in Junior College library innovations. The computer printout catalog and range of automated technical processes have been much refined over the exaggerated beginning three decades ago. We place less emphasis on hardware now, than they did then, largely because technology and the scientific method on which it is based is steadily declining in the face of the exciting implosions being caused by the startling discoveries in parapsychology Instead, our whole theory of learning has been disrupted by the marvels of telepathy, clairvoyance, precognition, and most recently, psychokinesis. Fast as we considered the computer before, it is now approaching horse and buggy status in the face of the instantaneous telepathic communication we have discovered we have within us, only awaiting individualized development. It is difficult for us to understand how scientists who prided themselves on openmindedness could have crucified such a breakthrough mind like that of the late, great Joseph Banks Rhine, of Duke University.

Perhaps the best way to understand 1969 is to look at their curriculum. There was a hierarchy of subjects. The natural sciences ruled the roost, with the physical sciences just a bit more respectable than the biological ones. Most of the humanities were given the respect that goes to old age. Philosophy resisted the sacred method of science, to some extent, but the arts and literature steadily abdicated to the dominant culture, and as for the social sciences they outdid each other to mimic the natural sciences. Sociology and education, particularly, because they had remained on the other side of the railroad track for so long in the academic community, often went to ludicrous quantitative extremes in their investigations. But what the curriculum suffered from most was a passionate commitment to specialism. If you had lived on a college campus then, as I did for four decades before retirement you would have been convinced that Genesis should have been, rewritten in terms of chemistry, mathematics, economics, psychology, grammar and the other subjects the academicians had established as prime.

The Junior College had a hard time. It had to begin by establishing three programs they called college parallel, terminal, and continuing. And these two-year upstarts had to swear on the Bible that never would these three programs be permitted to mix. Once a student was cast as a terminal he had to keep his place and get no upstart ideas about college parallel.

The Junior College changed this curriculum artificiality. And not too soon. For the United States was suffering from a shortage of carpenter, plumber, electrician, and other manual talents. It took the Junior College to restore the whole man and whole woman perspective. It insisted that every citizen had a manual obligation to his community. At the same time it recognized that citizenship was enhanced by offering everyone an opportunity at higher education in concepts and abstractions.

As a result the Junior College contributed a new curriculum perspective. Led by library media generalists it introduced the knowledge overview at the beginning, and the knowledge capstone synthesis at the end. These two courses, as you know, have become common requirements; the specialisms elective.

To reenforce the independent study learning mode the Junior College, again led by its media generalists, introduced an augmented course on Media, required of all students. If the half of knowledge is knowing where to find it, then the time had come to give some earnest attention to this half.

Finally, as a contribution to what 1969 liked to call the Generation Gap, an exaggeration even in 1969 when the gaps were even greater within the generations than between them, the Junior College introduced the idea that the Curriculum should consist not only of what is significant to the older generation but what is most significant to the younger generation. Thus again the Media Generalist showed the Junior College the way by introducing the Student Interest Profile. After the faculty indicated through syllabus, curriculum content considered significant by the older generation, students were invited to indicate in ranked order their deepest interests and greatest involvements no matter how inconsequential their elders might consider these. Student Profiles are weighed as heavily as faculty choices in Media selection.

Well, here we are in 1999 with another revolting younger generation. Those of us who wore beards in 1969, gloried in our love-ins, denounced the older generation as squares, liked to hear the demagogues among our elders sympathize with us for inheriting problems we didn't create, and were ready to march at the drop of a hat, now find it hard to tolerate the dissent of our own youth. We can't understand why they shave their heads, call music with a beat corny, like romanticism with happy endings, roar with laughter over realism, refuse to believe that their parents could have lined up for any movie as dull as *Bonnie and Clyde*. Perhaps they are nearer the truth than we. I seem to recall that there was a musical in our times called *Man of La Mancha* in which Don Quixote said, It takes less courage to describe things as they are, than as they should be.

LIBRARY-COLLEGE USA

PART THREE: LIBRARY-COLLEGE ELEMENTS

13.

THE LIBRARY-COLLEGE FACULTY

(Essay for the Founder's Week Faculty Meeting on the Silver Anniversary of the Orlando Junior College, Florida, April 26, 1966.)

HIGHER EDUCATION faces the greatest challenge and most strategic opportunity world history has ever recorded. The United States has committed itself to higher educate all its people. If the nation meets this commitment, perhaps for the first time, leaders and followers in a society will be able to communicate with each other in such a way as to preclude violent revolution.

But if the United States is to fulfill this commitment a radically different higher education must evolve. Evidence of changing higher education was dramatically presented in a colloquium at Wakulla Springs, Florida in the spring of 1964.[2]

At the top of the list of reported changes was reorganization to insure numerically small student bodies. Liberal arts colleges are striving for student populations under 1,000. Universities are moving toward the British cluster college pattern. The new University of California at Santa Cruz, for example, announced that its "colleges will vary from 250 to 1,000 students."[3] At the neighboring University of the Pacific President Burns decided:

> Let us grow larger by growing smaller. Let us develop about the University a cluster of colleges which will retain the values we cherish so much and yet will at the same time make it possible for us to accept some responsibility for educating the increasing number of young people seeking to enter institutions of higher learning . . . Let us follow the Oxford and Cambridge system and expand by establishing

> small, interrelated colleges clustered together to draw strength from each other and from the University as a whole.[4]

Michigan State University decided that as new residence dormitories were constructed each would house an experimental liberal arts college:

> ". . . with a distinctive program which would provide a common educational experience to all students in a single residence hall . . . The first three new halls . . . each houses 1200 students . . . include a total of 14 classrooms, six laboratories, 47 offices, an auditorium, a kiva, a library, and five conference rooms."[5]

Orlando might consider the cluster college idea to accommodate its gratifying enrollment increase, and at the same time, protect its personal attention to the student's education.[6] If the University of Orlando is activated there will be even more reason to establish several small colleges rather than attempt to handle the student body *en masse.*

But even more exciting than the cluster college movement were reports of variations on the independent study trend. Antioch has experimented with autonomous courses in which the student, after a preliminary lecture introducing the broad outlines of the subject and the sources, spends the term reading independently in the library. From time to time he confers with the instructor. When several students feel a need to discuss their readings, the instructor calls a class meeting.

At Florida Presbyterian College:

> The winter term is a special four to five week period of independent study . . . Designed to develop qualities of self-discipline in pursuits requiring the student to be the prime explorer, the winter term asks him to work without customary routine of classroom and lecture hall . . .[7]

Individualized student learning in the library is steadily replacing group teaching in the classroom as the educational mode. This is demanded by the national commitment to higher educate all people, for as college approaches the compulsory status, the range of student individual differences becomes ever wider. This widening range makes a classroom–focused education ever more untenable. By the nature of the group approach in the classroom the teacher's activity must be greatest. And he is confronted by the necessity of preparing a class plan which aims at the mythical average. Furthermore, as he lectures or leads the discussion, the most he can hope for is an intellectual passivity by the majority.

The classroom as a mode of learning is a persistent holdover from ancient and medieval days when the principal medium of communication was the master's oral communication of information to his pupils. Even after the invention of the printing press, books were so limited that the best the individual could hope for was a single textbook to supplement the teacher's lecture. It was not until this century that libraries began to develop in strength sufficiently to enable faculty to adopt reserve readings as a classroom assignment form. But the classroom contact as a measure of education persisted beyond World War I, despite frequent rebellions by both students and faculty.

Independent study has grown in popularity in undergraduate colleges. Even some high schools, like that at Ridgefield, Illinois, have moved to independent study, and an elementary school in Shaker Heights, Ohio, with a subsidy from the Ford Foundation, is experimenting in independent study.

Evidence is mounting of the passing of the classroom contact as the measure of learning. As libraries reach high standards of quality and quantity they can match individual differences in students with individual differences in instructional materials. The universe of library media is now so nearly universal in subject, format and level that it is entirely possible to customize learning so each learner can begin at his individual point of readiness.

What then is the role of the faculty? With enthusiasm I exclaim, more exciting than ever before. The college instructor can now do creative teaching that the outmoded lockstep of the medieval classroom precluded. He can begin to develop the individual mind, talent, and spirit of his students. The coming of the Library-College frees both the professor and student to undertake liberal education together.

In his new role the Library-College faculty member is a counsellor to the individual student. He maintains daily office hours not in excess of the time required presently by combined class meetings and student appointments. Less frequently, but as the situation demands, there are seminar or small group meetings. Once or twice a term each faculty member presents a lecture, open to any one in the college. The content should represent original investigation and contain information not readily available in library material. Because the lecture is not routinely delivered at a fixed hour three times a week it reflects the incentive and inspiration harnessed for the event. The essay may even be prepared for publication.

The Library-College faculty member is also a bibliographer extraordinary. He knows the literature of his subject so well that he can prescribe for the individual differences of his students as adroitly as the skilled physician diagnoses and treats his individual patients. To do this the faculty member must know each of his students individually. The instructor should be able to sense the young person's talents and limitations, to determine the point of readiness to learn. And then out of his intimate knowledge of the literature of his subject prescribe medium or media which will best start the youngster off toward the common goal.

Today there are many highly bibliographic faculty. Although no stereotype for this new breed of faculty member can possibly exist, here are some examples of library teaching.

In an Antioch Economics class the group came together for one hour on the opening day of the fall term. The professor talked briefly and informally about Economics as a subject. Then he handed out an overview which defined some of the terminology. A second handout was a basic bibliography of sources, classics, journals, learned societies, key publications, federal and state government agencies, movements and problems current in the subject, famous economists, and Dewey Decimal numbers among which to browse in the library. The third handout was a syllabus of a standard course in beginning Economics.

Said the professor:

> Now, you are on your own. The next time I see you will be when you want to see me. My office hours are at the bottom of your third stencil. There is also a calendar of minimum events. You owe me three written reports of progress at the times indicated. The forms for these reports are indicated on the reverse side of the third page. And there is a final day of reckoning. What will be required for that is also indicated. So long, and happy reading in the library.

There are many variations of independent study. For instance a professor may take his class to the library the first day and browse with them in the stacks. Another interesting approach has been to assign overview articles on the course subject from the major encyclopedias. Another way has been to open the subject with a controversial motion picture. Still another exciting opening has been entirely bibliographic, with annotations and displays of the basic reference sources for the subject.

Soon individuals begin to raise questions which arise from their reading. Here a concept may be unclear, so the Library-College faculty member begins his diagnosis by prescribing from his rich knowledge of the literature a precise format and level that will exactly match the individual's readiness. There a conflict may develop between two accents, or points of view, or even sets of facts. A subtle diagnosis is called for, related to the maturity as well as foundations the students bring to the situation. Perhaps the issue warrants a seminar or even a major essay-lecture by the professor.

It is apparent that the Library-College faculty must be extraordinarily equipped in bibliography. The library sophistication of this new breed professor must be beyond that of most college faculty. The professor who library teaches is known and revered by the librarian. In countless ways he who teaches with books reveals himself by the nature of his assignments, the library sophistication of his students, his current awareness of the literature output in his subject, and his orders for new materials.

As for library sophistication, a number of graduate schools are now offering courses in literature searching that go beyond undergraduate library orientation.[8] I recommend increased exploration of the library learning idea.

REFERENCES

1. As suggested in previous essays.
2. Stickler, W. Hugh, *Experimental Colleges.* Tallahassee, Florida State University, 1964. 185p.
3. *Ibid.*, pp. 133-44.
4. *Ibid.*, p. 75.
5. *Ibid.*, pp. 127-28.
6. Shores, Louis. "The Library Junior College" *Junior College Journal* (March 1966), pp. 6-9.
7. Stickler, *op. cit.*, pp. 96ff.
8. Shores, Louis. "Library Research and Reporting" *Collier's Encyclopedia.* 1965. Volume XIV, pp. 601-7.

14.

THE LIBRARY-COLLEGE LIBRARIAN

(Essay for the Tennessee Library Association, Nashville, May 12, 1967)

LIBRARIANS OF colleges and universities may spearhead the revolutionary changes ahead in our professional image. The reason why academic librarians may lead colleagues who perform in the other three library types—public, school, and special—is because Higher Education appears to be further ahead in innovational thinking than any of the other three communities served by our profession. This is said with considerable awareness of the computerized information designing in industrial and government libraries; of the media concept extensions in school libraries; the cooperative approaches in public library service, and other new dimensional undertakings. The advantage academic librarianship enjoys is the fast and furious college experimenting now under way, part of it hastened by the demonstrative campus unrest; part by the sudden confrontation of universal higher education, another U.S. first in world history.

If I cite only a half dozen recent conferences and movements it is because I have had an opportunity to be identified with them. Many more innovational efforts, possibly of greater significance, flourish in many sections of our nation. Beginning nearest home, Florida State University, with some subsidy from the Southern Regional Education Board, sponsored in the spring of 1964 a Colloquium of Experimental Colleges,[1] at Wakulla Springs. Among the ten experimenting institutions invited were four large state universities: the University of Michigan's Dearborne; Michigan State's Innovation colleges; Wayne State's Monteith; and the University of California's Santa Cruz. All of these multiversities were basically attempting to halt the growing impersonality of education's skyrocketing enrollments. In the words of President McHenry of Santa Cruz the purpose of the British university type organization now gaining favor:

> ". . . is to organize instruction in such a way that the advantages of a small college—close, instruction, sense of belonging, residential setting—are combined with those of a large university—great scholars, excellent libraries and laboratories, and superior cultural events. We hope in this way to help bridge the gap between the curricular and co-curricular and to fill in the chasm that so often yawns between student and faculty."

As academic librarians we must ponder first the implications for our role in this trend toward close instruction.

In the remaining six colleges reporting their experiments at the Wakulla Colloquium—Antioch, Stephens, Parsons, Pacific, Florida Presbyterian, and New—where close instruction because of small enrollments is less of a problem, the dominant innovation involves independent study. Whether labelled honors reading, or autonomous courses, or just independent study the learning mode reverses the conventional relation between classroom instruction and library learning by making the former supportive to the latter. At least 100 colleges and universities in the United States, now, have committed themselves to this innovation in varying degrees, and nearly all other institutions of higher education are examining its potential, including the growing number of junior colleges. All of us in academic libraries are, of course, redoubling our ancillary efforts in acquisition, classification, cataloging, circulation, and conservative reference in response to this innovation. But should we not also reexamine our professional role in terms of new dimensions, with comparable approaches of innovation?

Although academic librarianship as a comprehensive term embracing service to all kinds of colleges and university libraries is being increasingly used by library schools to identify this type of professional commitment, neither our dictionaries nor our basic textbooks uses this terminology. Drawing from the contributions of the three textbooks I have used most of my library school study and teaching—Randall, Lyle, Wilson and Tauber—I offer here this definition of *academic librarianship*: that branch of the profession of librarianship concerned with the acquisition, processing, dissemination, housing, and management of the book resources, in all formats, necessary to support instruction and research in colleges and universities. I underline "in all formats" because some of you may not recall my long struggle to gain recognition for so-called audio-visual formats as part of my philosophical concept of the "generic" book.[3]

Please understand I am not recommending that we discontinue our responsibilities of the past. There is no reason for feeling insecure about our work or to resist educational innovation as a threat to our livelihood. What I am asking is that we reexamine our objectives against the new perspectives and in some cases startling implications of these trends to close instruction in our multiversities, and independent study in all institutions of higher education. Specifically, if these two innovations point inevitably to the passing of the classroom as the symbol of education, what happens to our predominant professional objective of supporting classroom instruction? Do we merely transfer our support to individual independent study in our library carrels or do we at long last assert ourselves by developing an educational program of our own?

If you will go back to the proceedings of the A.L.A. 1934 Chicago Century of Progress convention you will find there a report of my "Library-Arts College" paper, subsequently published in *School and Society*. It proposed a new kind of college—a college which is entirely a library and in which the learning mode was independent study bibliographically guided and inspired by a new breed faculty member—a cross between the library-minded classroom instructor and the educationally-minded college librarian.[4] Although periodically restated and cited before and after World War II the idea languished until a new apostle, Robert Jordan, aided by fellow disciples launched a movement of their own which they renamed the "Library-College," with a hyphen between the two words. In 1962 a College Talkshop was held at Kenyon College and the nucleus of an informal organization initiated among the disciples. The monthly *Library-College Newsletter* was launched under Robert T. Jordan as editor-in-chief, and each issue under a rotating editor.[5]

The Wakulla Colloquium, although not entirely devoted to the Library-College idea, was partly the result of continuing the Kenyon beginning, and it devoted considerable attention to aspects of the movement. It was followed by the Syracuse conference of June 1965 on the "Library and the College Climate for Learning." A Library-Colleger, Dan Bergen, assisted by such fellow disciples as Bob Jordan and Pat Knapp, out-innovated a behavioral sociologist, a psychologist, and a higher educationist in his symposium.[6] Then in December 1965 an entire conference was devoted for the first time to the Library-College when President Dan Sillers of Jamestown (N.D.) College boldly decided to activate a prototype there.[7]

The Jamestown Workshop attracted some 40 college presidents, deans, professors, librarians, government and foundation specialists, and college student leaders. After a review of the idea generally, in literature, and in papers prepared by the participants especially for the Workshop, the conference settled down to designing specifically for the Jamestown campus a Library-College. Elements in this design can be found in part three of the book, *The Library-College*. From the Jamestown Charter, developed by the Workshop, I quote:

> "The purpose of the Library-College is to increase the effectiveness of student learning particularly through the use of library-centered independent study with a bibliographically expert faculty."[8]

Although the May 1966 Innovation conference held at Magnolia, Massachusetts under the joint sponsorship of the Association of Experimental Colleges and the U.S. Office of Education considered aspects, only, of the Library-College idea it was significant for the movement. For not only was the concept brought to the attention of some 40 college presidents of institutions in the vanguard of experimenting, as well as foundational, associational, and governmental leaders, but the Jamestown Charter was further refined.[9] Among the colleges reporting on their experiment was Oklahoma Christian with its new library building seating 110% of its student body at one time in carrels that could be designated as "wet." Each student has his exclusive work bench, where he can lock his belongings, and for which he pays $30 a semester. Each wet carrel is electronically equipped to dial tape recordings of music, missed professors' lectures, other sounds and voices.[10] "The fundamental objective," says Dean Stafford North "Is to give every student his own 'private study' . . . the philosophy of a college education has long suggested that most of a student's learning should take place outside of the classroom . . ."

Last December, Drexel Institute staged an entire conference devoted to the Library-College. The response was surprising. Over 200 college presidents, deans, professors, librarians, registered. The keynote address[11] by Chancellor emeritus of Vanderbilt University, Dr. Harvie Branscomb, on Sunday night challenged librarians again as he had in his classic study for the Carnegie Corporation in 1940,[12] *Teaching With Books*, when he wrote:

> "To sum it up, it may be said without hesitation that the fundamental need of the college library is to develop a distinctive program of its own. Absorbed as it has been in the task of increasing its supply of books and compelled to serve constantly increasing student body . . . it has been too imitative of other institutions.

The Drexel Conference accepted Chancellor Branscomb's challenge and presented in subsequent sessions variations on the Library-College theme. Pending the publication of the full Drexel proceedings, scheduled for 1967 release, briefs and summaries can be read in the *Library-College Newsletter*, number eleven. Distinctive programs, college library initiated and designed can be found in the book, *The Library-College*. Let it be understood here that there is no one *Library-College* design. There is only consensus on the central idea that the college is fundamentally a library where the student studies independently under the bibliographic guidance and stimulation of the faculty. As you read the book *The Library-College* you will discover that there is a Jordan Library-College; and a Sillers version; a North American Library College by William Hinchliff; and among others, something named by Bob Jordan the Shores Library-College.

Obviously I am best prepared to describe this last named prototype. But let me hasten to say that college is by no means in its final form. I am still rethinking aspects of it. And I readily credit my stimulating colleagues in the movement, like B. Lamar Johnson, who wrote that classic of academic librarianship some years ago, when he held the unique combined position at Stephens of Dean-Librarian, for later adjustments in my design. I owe great debts to Stafford North at Oklahoma Christian; to Bob Gaylor at Oakland University; to Tom Minder of IBM; to Ted Samore, formerly of

U.S.O.E., and now at the University of Wisconsin; to Sister Helen (Sheehan), Trinity College, Washington, D. C.; to Presidents Dan Sillers of Jamestown College and John Tirrell of Oakland Community College; and of course Pat Knapp of Monteith and now of Wayne State Library School and Robert Jordan of the Council on Library Resources. Shortly the movement will have its own quarterly journal, to be named *Innovation,* to be sponsored by The Library-College Associates, organized in Philadelphia, December 1966, to be published at the University of the State of New York in Brockport, and edited by Howard Clayton. This is the movement. Now for one design.

In my concept I consider the Library-College Librarian key to the idea. He (or she) must be committed to education above management. Remember I do not say we can do without management. A badly managed library would be a handicap to the whole idea. But a librarian who subordinated education to management would be fatal to this distinctive program of the college library's very own.

How is management subordinated to education by the college library? Let me try to describe something that does not fully exist yet, except in my mind's eye, and in embryo among the studies and projects exploring cooperative efforts between classroom faculty and library faculty. If I were a librarian again, as I once was, of a small college I would try to find a classroom faculty colleague who taught either my undergraduate major— English, or my graduate interest—history, or even an entirely foreign subject for me, who was keen on educational experimenting. With college consent we would agree to set up two control groups, one to follow the conventional classroom instruction with supportive library work. The other group of students to undertake the Library-College learning mode, which reverses the conventional relationship between classroom and library.

On the first day of class my colleague and I would begin with our students to build a curriculum. We would do this with some library approaches and techniques which my classroom faculty colleague would know from well to not at all. He would present a syllabus and readings that traditionally covered the content of this subject. I, the librarian would present a stencil covering the subject based on the following: 1. Library classifications D.C. and L.C.; 2. Encyclopedias A, B, C (*Americana, Britannica, Collier's*).

The students would present without restriction the subjects in life that interest them most, in ranked order. These three presentations would constitute the beginning of curriculum construction.

One week without classes would then be devoted to individual independent study in the student's exclusive work bench, his own carrel. The common assignment would be to develop, in this case, a content for this course that would enable the student to match his fellow students in conventional classes on evaluative final examinations or tests or papers and at the same time give considerable attention to the personal interests he rated high. Faculty counseling by librarian and classroom exponent would be available to students individually and in small groups.

The second class meeting would be devoted to finalizing the syllabus for the course. Topics would be ranked in two columns of priorities: 1. conventionally required for this course and necessary to comply with standardized tests; 2. individual interests. For these two lists of topics sources would be explored. Here again the librarian would lead, reviewing as glamorously as possible the rich and faculty-student neglected reference books on the open shelves, first. Then in order would come format, subject and level approaches to the collection. These three considerations for the browsing week ahead would cover for format the use of not only the hard cover and paper back, the periodical and document, but the globe and map, the picture and object, but the slide, transparency, filmstrip; microtext, microprojection, motion picture; disc, tape; radio and its transcription; television and its videotape or kine. For these are the format components of the generic book. So also are examples of programmed materials, computer assisted instructional media; and of course, the community resources, natural, social and human. If I have omitted any other format know that a larger representation can be found in my book, *Instructional Materials*.[13]

The other two approaches to the collection are more common with us in librarianship. Our library classifications offer a guide to what we know as well as a subject index to the library. But it does more than that, educationally. The study of library classification by college students, not as we frequently teach in library use instruction for freshmen where the accent is our own library school orientation for practicing the profession, is for subject perspective. D.C., L.C., Bliss, and other classifications expose what we know is an overview. From the first summary into the complete tables,

Dewey, which it is now so professionally fashionable to satirize, reveals an overview of knowledge. In addition it relates the segmentations our campus specialists currently isolate, labor union-like, to the confusion of the freshman and the frustration of the senior. And it delves into the interstices our predatory campus instructional departments fiercely forbid, some times.

As for the level approaches, it is vital to the Library-College independent study learning mode. The student must begin individually where he now is and proceed at the pace his background and talent support. You will recall when we made much of something we called ladder lists. Well, these, and something we have called browsing combine to give us a learning mode of our own; an answer to Dr. Branscomb's challenge that we stop imitating others and find a pattern that distinctly belongs to the college library rather than to the college classroom.

And so the student moves into something we call book selection, or in today's terminology, media selection. This is distinctly library, not classroom. Selection has an educational potential not quite recognized by our classroom colleagues whose own library-college days were almost criminally negligent in literature searching, or source study *per se*. And the student undertakes the process delightfully with our own innovation, browsing. Here is a whole week at least set aside for exploring the stacks; for dialing at the wet carrel among a variety of formats; for field trips to community resources; for the purpose of developing an individually tailored bibliography to accompany the list of topics compiled the previous week. And book selection for the library enters when the student as well as the faculty discover lacunae in the library collection for the topics of the syllabus.

By the fourth week the student gets down to intensive reading, listening, viewing, yes and smelling, tasting, touching. But most importantly comes extrasensory perception, which I am convinced is the basis of what Count Keyserling once called creative understanding. One day our pragmatic concepts of education based almost exclusively today on physical psychology will move into parapsychology, and the martyrdom of J. B. Rhine at Duke will be sanctified. As a prelude to such extrasensory learning the library offers that hard to find these days quiet for meditation. In this, too, is a library learning opportunity unimitative of the classroom climate of group lockstepping, of imitating Pepsi adoration of where the action is.

Evaluation, the crux of the learning matter, follows conventional as well as some innovative models. As at Florida Presbyterian's winter inter term, where all classes are replaced for a month to six weeks by library reading, topic papers are the end results and the measure. But there are other evaluations: conference with faculty; seminar discussions; performances of all kinds, dramatic, musical, athletic, manipulative. And finally there are the conventional tests and examinations on which both controlled groups must register.

This beginning of the Library-College learning mode in a conventional college classroom setting obviously does not represent the Library-College models designed by several of us. But it exposes some elements of an educational design, already in the college library, but for the most part supportive to classroom instruction. What is suggested by this specific beginning is what Dr. Branscomb challenges: an educational concept and design that is not ancillary, but initiatory. What we have here is the start of an education in which the classroom-teaching device is ancillary or supportive of the library-learning mode. The advantages we have over the classroom-centered education is that ours is more student-centered; their's more teacher-centered. Inherent in classroom teaching is group communication pitched at the mythical average of college intelligence. Frequently this overwhelms the less talented; frustrates the gifted. Library learning, characterized by individual, independent study in a carrel, whether dry or wet, is customized to individual differences. And believe me this becomes ever more important as emerging universal higher education confronts those of us who gladly teach with the widest range of individual differences our colleges have ever known.

So let me join Chancellor Branscomb in this challenge to the college librarian. The time has come for us in librarianship to stop "imitating other institutions" and create our own. I offer such a creation in the Library-College. I propose that we enter into this vast innovative revival now underway on our restless campus, not only in a supportive role but in an initiatory way with our own educational concepts and patterns. I suggest that we begin on our conventional campuses, with or without federal grants, to explore with our classroom colleagues the relative educational effectiveness of classroom teaching and library learning. But I insist at least some of these explorations should be librarian initiated with the classroom in the ancillary, supportive role.

If this is to be done it must be started by the librarian, not by the classroom teacher. And it must be started by a librarian boldly willing to break with the past. It must be started by the Library-College Librarian.

REFERENCES

1. Sticklers, W. Hugh. Experimental Colleges; Their Role in American Higher Education. 1964. 185p.
2. McHenry, D. E. (In *Experimental Colleges.* 1964. p. 136)
3. Shores, Louis. "Books—Continuous Communicability." *Saturday Review.*
4. "The Library-Arts College" *School and Society,* 1935. v. 41, p. 110-14. (Reprinted for *The Library-College.* 1966. p.34)
5. The *Library-College Newsletter,* 1965, no. 1 (monthly).
6. Bergen, Dan and Duryea, E. D. *Libraries are the College Climate of Learning.* 1966. 84p. (see Review, *L.J.* 92:1426 Ap. '67)
7. *The Library-College,* ed. by Louis Shores, Robert T. Jordan, John Harvey. 1966. 287p.
8. *Ibid.* p.IX
9. Magnolia, Massachusetts.
10. North, Stafford. "Learning Center Gives Each Student a Study Carrel." *College and University Business.* 1966, May.
11. *The Library College Newsletter.* no. 11, ed. by Louis Shores. January, 1967. p.2.
12. Branscomb, Harvie. *Teaching With Books.* 1940, p. 9.
13. Shores, Louis. *Instructional Materials.* 1960, 370p.

15.

THE LIBRARY-COLLEGE LIBRARY

(Essay for the national conference of the Catholic Library Association, St. Paul, Minnesota, April 1968. Published *Catholic Library World,* 1968, 40:103-8)

THE TREND TO independent study in the United States' Higher Education presages the inevitability of the Library-College as the American College of the near future.

When a college is a library, and a library is a college, it is a Library-College. In the Library-College, group teaching to students in classrooms is subordinated to individual learning in library carrels. A faculty's role becomes largely that of a bibliographic counselor who matches individual differences in students with individual differences in media. The Library-College, aspects of which can be found in nearly 100 experimental colleges, owes its inspiration to Thomas Carlyle's essay on the "Hero as Man of Letters" which appeared in *Heroes and Hero Worship,* published about 1848. In this essay the words occur that are so often quoted: "The true university is a collection of books."

Just as the Library-College causes changes in the students' learning mode, and in the faculty's teaching role, so it calls for some new dimensions in the library itself. The Library-College library differs from the conventional library in these elements: stock, housing, personnel, and function.

A Library-College library is stocked with the *Generic Book.* This means that not only hard and soft cover print are included in the collection, but film and transparencies; discs and tapes; radio and television; indexes to community resources; programmed learning materials—print, machine, electronic, and computer; and a whole range of graphic and other media formats. Not only is there a range of formats as a means of matching individual differences in students; but there is also a spread of difficulty to correspond with the levels of maturity found in the learners. And of course, all the subjects of the current college curriculum, plus the student's co-curricular interests, and an interdisciplinary approach that has not yet been accomplished by our segmented departments and courses are attempted.

The Library-College library building departs radically from today's architecture by providing individual seating for 100% of the student body. In his carrel, the student has dial access to a wide range of media formats, levels, and subjects. Around him are faculty offices for conference and counsel. There are also seminars for group meetings, and a few larger rooms for lectures, recitals, film showings, theater performances, etc.

Released from much of the routine, that has so long chained the professional librarian, by (1) automation; (2) a new level of library worker now called technician, the librarian, at long last, takes his role of destiny—teaching with the *Generic Book.* His teaching innovation introduces into the educational bloodstream (1) that half of knowledge is knowing where to find it; (2) the other half which is the *gestalt* of interdisciplines. Also, he furthers independence in the learning mode by his techniques of browsing and of ladder lists.

With this overview of the Library-College, let's explore some dimensions.

THE GENERIC BOOK

To develop the book stock, the Library-College library takes a new approach in its selection. Selection becomes *Generic Book* selection. I mean by the *Generic Book* what I wrote in the editorial of the *Saturday Review*[1] on the occasion of the First National Library Week. Generic means a class of related things; and genus means similars. The hierarchy of classification puts genus just above the species. In addition to these general definitions, let me add one quotation taken from Webster's *Dictionary of Synonyms,*[2] "The word generic is used commonly in reference to ideas, emotions, passions, moods, conditions, or the like, that have a traceable cause or source; as a habit of thought . . . only to be generated by intimate knowledge of good literature." To this is added the quotation from Inge: "I do not think religious feeling is ever aroused, except by ideas, objectives truth and value; these ideas are certainly not generated by feeling."

Now I will define the *Generic Book* as I understand it: All the means of communication, not only between man and his earthly environment, but also with God.

Consequently, the *Generic Book* includes all the sensory media we know, not only the hard cover print we have come to call the book, but other formats, the picture and the motion picture; the tape and the disc; the transparency overlay, whether it is projected by an overhead projector, or whether it is included within the covers of an encyclopedia. The *Generic Book* includes, in addition, all the newer machine and electronic media, sometimes referred to as programmed materials, or even teaching machines. It includes all the means of communication shared by what we now call Computer Assisted Instruction. There are within the *Generic Book* concept scattered species of community resources, school journeys or field trips; museum objects, which audio-visualists fancily sometime call *Realia*; boards of all kinds, felt, peg, flannel, magnetic; dioramas, puppets, marionettes, perhaps a hundred other formats which might be considered subspecies, and which I have identified in my book *Instructional Materials.*[3]

If we accept this definition of the *Generic Book*, you can understand why the term used by some librarians, "non-book materials," has always been anathema to me. Because the word *book*, in my opinion, is a comprehensive term which covers what we have lately called Media. To be a bit philosophical, there was in my *Saturday Review* editorial, the story about the French general in World War I.

Those of us who engage in war, first-hand, know that Western man's reluctance to discuss or even consider the subject of death is released on the war front. There, one cannot escape meditation and contemplation. One moment you are talking to your closest buddy in a foxhole, in a trench, on the street. The next moment a bullet, or exploding shrapnel has taken him away. This concern is illustrated by the question a soldier asked his general in World War I.

"General, what is death?" This general is said to have thought for a moment and then replied, "Death is sudden incommunicability." The General's reply defined death especially well for that soldier. Suddenly the buddy is no longer able to communicate. This is death.

The French General did something more for me. He not only defined death. He defined for me the meaning of life. For if death is incommunicability; then life must be communicability. Of all the ways in which mankind communicates and gives evidence of life, a composite book is a record of civilization. Basically, therefore, the *Generic Book* gives evidence of life. This is the reason why our professional librarianship is such a basic profession in man's existence. This is why I have so often spoken and written about our profession of destiny.

A part of that destiny is to educate mankind. In 1940, Chancellor Harvie Branscomb of Vanderbilt University wrote in his classic Carnegie Study, entitled *Teaching With Books,* these challenging words:

> "To sum up, it may be said without hesitation that the fundamental need of the college library is to develop a distinctive program of its own."[4]

The essence of the library's own education is in the concept of the *Generic Book.* Librarianship must begin to look at the *Generic Book* as encompassing all formats, all levels, all subjects. Basically, the Library-College library introduces new principles of book selection in a three-fold approach. First of all, the Library-College library accepts other formats than the hard cover print without apology and without condescension. These are not non-book materials. They are book materials. There is an educational concept in the cross-media approach to *Generic Book* selection.

Those of us who have taught for many years, both in the classroom and in the reading room, are aware that the format of the media may influence a learning situation. In the whole furor about Marshall McLuhan, *The Obscurities and Spectaculars,* of his hour long television program, there is one fundamental truth he has not communicated too simply at times, as *Understanding Media*[5] would suggest.

Let me illustrate with these few examples. In elementary through library school, I have at various times taught about the making of paper, so essential to a book. If some students could read about the process and understand it; others could not. So we reinforced reading with a visit to a paper mill. Teachers who have engaged in field trips and school journeys with children and older students know the advantages in the community resource as a medium of communication. They also know the disadvantages. In a class of 30, perhaps as many as six will aggressively push themselves forward to see the actual operation being described by the guide. At least twice that many students, diffident for one reason or another, or because of the limited space, can't get very close, and either lose significant points, or become totally disinterested. This was embarrassingly illustrated when a fourth grade teacher asked a pupil in the class after a school journey,

"Johnny, what was the most interesting thing you saw at the water plant we visited yesterday?"

Johnny replied, "The little yellow dog that came up to us on the way to the water plant."

Reading, and a visit to the paper mill, communicate to only about half of the class. The teacher or the good librarian who is essentially a teacher, tries other formats. I know of at least two good motion pictures on papermaking. With these, the camera is able to focus on the process, bringing it close to all students. The guide's voice is clearly audible all over the room. It has been proven that some students learn better about paper making in a film than through either reading or from a visit to the paper mill. This way individual differences in pupils are matched with individual differences in media formats.

Another example. Since modern foreign language teaching has now shifted its former exclusive accent on grammar, reading, and writing, and introduced at least an equal emphasis on speaking, teachers have been desperately trying to help students speak like natives. No matter how much their critical marks and accents are used with textbooks, these devices are not sufficient for speaking a language as people from that country do. There are certain nuances, raising and lowering of the voice, that disturb and frustrate American students who study French and make their first visit to Paris; the student of Spanish who arrives in a Latin American country for the first time.

We have for some time known that disc recordings, played over and over again, provide a better format than the printed page for learning native pronunciation. In Florida, where we are very close to Latin America, and where Spanish is the most popular of all modern foreign languages, students in our schools have made dramatic use of another format, the tape. Part of an exchange we call

Operation Amigo is not only an exchange of students, bodily, between Columbia and Florida, for example, but in addition, is also an exchange of tapes. These tapes record Latin American high school students' discussion of subjects that do not so often find their way into textbooks; subjects of greatest concern to teenagers. American high school students record on tape similar conversations, probably with much of the slang attributed to the younger generation. I submit that here is a more effective way to learn pronunciation of foreign language.

Perhaps these two examples will help us to illustrate the reason for replacing hard cover book selections with *Generic Book* selection in the Library-College library.

Besides format, in *Generic Book* selection, another criterion is the level of maturity in the community served. The Library-College I advocate means college for everyone. Philosophically I will debate this with the Robert Maynard Hutchins School of Elitism. The debates go back at least as far as 1948, at the Graduate Library School, University of Chicago Institute, where I dissented with Dr. Clarence Faust's position. I believe in higher education for all, for several fundamental reasons. Historically, I believe a case can be made that violent revolution occurs when the higher educated leaders no longer communicate with the non-higher educated followers. I understand that the president of a multi-versity with some 40,000 students, when asked recently, "How many students do you have on your campus?" replied, condescendingly, "Only about 10%." Possibly so. But in my opinion the university is more to blame than the students for not discovering the individual gifts of those high school graduates admitted, and doing something to stimulate and develop the aptitudes present.

Generic Book selection by levels of maturity and aptitude found in the student body is one way. These levels can be discovered by a number of devices not entirely new to librarians. For example, on one campus where I am consultant, we have just completed something I labelled "Operation Bookcheck," which involved the entire faculty in a critical comparison of the library's holdings with the California basic list for a college library, department by department. When a faculty member dissented with a California selection for his subject, he was permitted to substitute his preference.

Following this faculty involvement in *retrospective* selection, a *current* awareness program was undertaken. This began with the construction of a Faculty Interest Profile. Each faculty member was asked to indicate his current research, instructional and hobby interests. On the basis of faculty responses, a subject index to faculty interests was compiled, and continuously updated. Against this index, or Faculty Interest Profile, library staff members check systematically current bibliographies and reviews in all subjects, formats, levels, represented.

It is now proposed to parallel this with a Student Interest Profile. As counterparts for the faculty research, instruction and hobby interests, it is contemplated that students will be asked each term to indicate vocational, course and hobby interests. This profile, too, will help shape *Generic Book* selection. It will provide a guide not only to the subject interests of students, curricular and co-curricular, but to the level of their maturity. Current awareness for students will be communicated not only through the usual media of bulletin boards, exhibits and displays, student paper, etc., but through individualized memoranda, personal counselling and library sponsored seminars, previews and pre-auds of tapes, discs and other sound formats.

THE FACILITY

To house the *Generic Book* and the independent study use that will be made of it increasingly, the Library-College will most certainly introduce some new dimensions into library architecture. In terms of site, universities may now have to think of cluster colleges, if intimate faculty and student relations are to be recaptured, and therefore, of multiple sites. California's Santa Cruz, for example, contemplating an ultimate student population of 27,500, plans to create a number of colleges on campus, Cambridge-Oxford like, no one of the colleges to have more than 1,000 students. Michigan State is experimenting with dormitory-centered colleges, each of which will have its own library. Hence, institutions with several thousand students may turn to multiple sites for their college libraries, plus a central site for the university graduate and research library.

But the most startling innovations will come in the planning of three fundamental accommodations for a library building. Stock accommodation, for example, can no longer plan for so-called audio-visual materials and equipment as an addition. These formats of the *Generic Book* must now be considered integral in facility planning.

READER ACCOMMODATION

The new dimension in Reader Accommodation for the Library-College library is an individual carrel for every student. Time was when as few as 15% of the student body to be seated at one time was an acceptable standard. This steadily advanced to 25%, and upward even to 50%, in a few new buildings. Oklahoma Christian has provided 110%, to allow for expansion. I consider a work bench of one's own as essential to the Library-College student as his exclusive toothbrush.

Of course, I am aware of the objections—economic, and even Gallup-Poll, like the recent *C. & R.L.* article.[6] The study there, reported by the psychologist, only serves to confirm the growing distrust of questionnaire-based investigations. Perhaps some students work best in their dormitory room, interrupted every other minute by conversations about styles, boy friends, or about football, girls, and the summer job. There may be a suggestion of discipline in the idea of a place marked specifically for work. But it is stretching the opposition by implying that an individual carrel prohibits study also in the recreation units with radio broadcasting the latest beat; or even with the television illustrating the newest twitch to accompany it.

Let's face it. At least some of the dropouts are victims of a life committed to "where the action is." One pastor told me recently on the plane that a girl who had been nearly a straight A student in high school failed in her first term at the state university. After considerable probing it was clear that the girl could find no quiet place to study. There were three other girls in her dormitory complex. The library was too small for the exploding student population, so that a seat, even at a table was a precious commodity. When the girl heard that there were college libraries where each student had his own carrel, her face lighted up. I sympathize with her. As a student in college I would have traded just about anything for a work bench I could call my own.

Increasingly, these carrels will become "wet." That is, they will have dial access to more and more media formats, visual as well as audial. These will include canned lectures, missed or wanted for review; language, literature, music, sounds of all kinds, transmitted from a central point in the library. It will include, also, an increasing number of visuals by means of inventions like LDX, telefacsimile, closed circuit TV, and who knows what else. This means that carrels built 'dry,' now, must provide outlets for eventual dial access. Indeed, the audio tutorial laboratory pioneered by Professor Postlethwaite at Purdue may eventually replace the traditional laboratory, for which James Thurber, Upton Sinclair and I have always had an allergy.

At Dallas Baptist College, where I have served as a library consultant, the architect and I have explored an idea for a square building with three major divisions. An inner core will house the stock, including shelves for printed books, files, cabinets, and other accommodations for the various formats and their equipment. Surrounding the stock will be student carrels, one for each student in the college. Surrounding the student carrels will be the third accommodation, that for staff. In this case, however, staff will include not only present library staff, but a new breed of librarians and faculty; their offices and work rooms, seminar, conference and classrooms; lecture hall and auditorium; and perhaps laboratories, too.

PERSONNEL

The Library-College will require, as you anticipate, a new breed faculty, a sort of cross between classroom instructors who teach with books, and librarians who are willing to be relieved of those duties which have made our professional image less attractive to the college graduates we seek to recruit. Considering the professional librarian first, relief from semiprofessional and clerical tasks are coming from two sources. One of these is technology and automation, although I am hopeful that we are now ready for more discriminating appraisal of hardware. I know at least one library where the librarian told me confidentially, "It takes longer, and costs more, but we are automated and our budget for other things has been greatly increased. The reason is because the president comes to the library more often so he can exhibit the gadgets to important visitors." But there are places where electronics have helped us immeasurably. I have high hopes for the return of the book catalog via computer printout, for example. The trend to central processing and to increasing inter-library cooperation will relieve professional personnel from unprofessional chores.

But a significant release will come from the new middle level personnel, the category the A.L.A. Interdivisional Committee has redesignated *Library Technical Assistant.*[7] Job descriptions have already been written by the U.S. Civil Service Commission in its GS-1411 series.[8] Texas, on a state-wide basis is even now developing syllabi for the courses to be offered in its junior colleges for the training of Library Technical Assistants,[9] as well as some other states, including California.[10]

Relieved of these duties, what will the Library-College Librarian do most? He will teach. He will help his Library-College develop the prototype for American higher education. He will do this because he will at long last realize that Carlyle's words "The true university is a collection of books" stands for a whole new concept of higher education made possible by contemporary implosions, as well as explosions. The principal explosion is being caused by the student revolt; chiefly against the classroom lockstep. An equally compelling explosion is resulting from the junior college movement, and the trend toward universal higher education. Inevitably, this is bringing the widest range of individual differences into the classroom, the widest that has ever been known. As a result, group-average student teaching in the classroom is becoming steadily less effective.

The librarian and the Library-College have some explosions of their own. There are now so many different instructional materials in format, level, and subject, that for the first time in the history of education, individual differences in students can be matched with individual differences in materials. This is the librarian's high mission in education. It is increasingly becoming the aim of good classroom teachers. This learning calls for independent study, individually guided by faculty who know media as well as they know their students.

I believe in college for all. But I believe this college must be individualized for our growing student population in the way it is not now, generally. The vehicle for this individualization is independent study in a library carrel. The American Higher Education of the future will inevitably assume a form like the Library-College.

REFERENCES

1. "Books: Continuous Communicability." *Saturday Review.*

2. *Webster's Dictionary of Synonyms.* 1942. p. 379.
3. *Instructional Materials.* Ronald, 1960. Chap. 2 .
4. Branscomb. Harvie. Teaching With Books. 1940. p. 9.
5. McLuhan, Marshall. *Understanding Media.*
6. Carrels. *College and Research Libraries.*
7. A.L.A. Interdivisional Committee. Guidelines. *A.L.A. Bulletin.* April, 1968.
8. U.S. Civil Service Commission. GS-1411 Series. 1966.
9. *Tex-Tec.* Syllabi for the Education of Library Technical Assistants. 1968. (In Process)
10. California. Library Technician. 1968.

16.

MEDICAL LIBRARY-COLLEGE

(Essay for the "Health Professionals," Mayo Auditorium, University of Minnesota Health Sciences Center, Minneapolis, August 29, 1969.)

I SPEAK WITH YOU as my peers in education. We who teach, gladly and sadly, at whatever level in any academic or professional area, confront, together, a world of learning in revolt. Whether in Town, or in Gown, protesters are marching everywhere. Too many of them prefer to communicate physically, rather than intellectually. They identify problems *ad nauseam*; abhor solutions. Most of these demonstrators are not students at all. But those who are legitimately enrolled in institutions of higher education must cause us, who attempt to teach them to pause and to ponder.

Recently, I have reread your Hippocratic Oath, a noble document, both in its original form, and as it was modified in 1948, in Geneva, by the General Assembly of the World Medical Association. From this latter form, I quote the part of the Oath that pertains to the student's responsibility to his teacher:

> I will give to my teachers the respect and gratitude which is their due.

I ask, have we earned this gratitude and respect? You from your students who are now practicing the various arts of the Health Sciences; I from my four decades of graduate students who are now practicing the various arts of the library sciences, which include segments especially important to you, like medical librarianship, information science, and bibliotherapy, among others.

It is fashionable these days, among protesters, to denounce

something called the Establishment. Inevitably, you have an Establishment in the Health Sciences; I have an Establishment in the Library Sciences; and the Demonstration, even though they may not admit it, already have an Establishment of their own which begins to be identified with certain male hair-do's. The denunciation, more often than not, of late has manifested itself in marches, or sit-ins, or take-overs of academic buildings—a new brand of so-called democratic action, a sort of promise of the society to come, in which if you do not conform with the new party line you will be snubbed, threatened, walker-out-on, or worse your library or your house may be burned or your teeth kicked in; or your relatives threatened, all in the name of their kind of liberation.

With these non-violent, violent elements in both our students and faculty there is no possibility of dialog. Let it only be noted there is no generation gap among them. The 19-year old draft dodger burns his draft card no more vigorously than a 60-year old doctor of Philip Wylie's term "momism." If they were inclined to document and debate instead of to demonstrate and destroy it could easily be proved they are protesting the half of the war which has more cause.

Our concern is with the quiet and thoughtful majority of both students and our faculty who are genuinely concerned with educational reform; who not only identify problems, but dialog, experiment, and innovate with solutions. While the noisy minority engage in exhibitionism, capture the time and space of our mass media, destroy and desicate, and even defecate in their professors' waste baskets, others carry on heroically, against inexcusable obstacles, the intellectual life of an academic community. I will summarize my dissent with the current dissent by pointing to history. If George Orwell's dread *1984* really does come about in the United States then this noisy part of our protest must assume the full blame for the abridgement of democracy that follows. If it does not, it will be because the dialog, documentation, experimentation and innovation of the quiet majority of our academic communities finally asserts itself and prevails.

Turning then to the generations also together who are in intellectual revolt against our schools and colleges we find considerable grounds for dissatisfaction with the dimensions of our education, on all levels, from pre-school through graduate school; in the so-called pure disciplines, and in the applied sciences and arts, many of which prepare for our professions. Before we consider, specifically, professional education in the Health Sciences let us examine the disaffections toward the general educations that must precede.

It would take too long to summarize the criticisms of our elementary and secondary schools. To save time let us begin with the campus revolt. Some recent Gallup-like education polls among college students exposed, in order, these dissatisfactions: one, the growing impersonality of higher education on our multiversity campuses in particular; two, the lockstep mode of class contact as a measure of learning; three, a rigid curriculum of predatory disciplines.

When the president of one of our multiversities that had just passed the 40,000 enrollment figure was recently asked how many students do you now have, he is reported to have replied, sarcastically, "oh, about 10%." He was reflecting the school of elitism thought, that the 90% of the population were not higher educable. I happen to disagree. I believe in our courageous first in the world college for all. As far back as 1948 you will find my dissent with the "elitist" position in my paper at the University of Chicago where one of Robert M. Hutchins' chief disciples, Dr. Clarence Faust and I read papers on opposite sides. I can only briefly indicate the philosophical basis for my position. There is some evidence in the history of nations that violent revolution occurs when the 10% higher educated can no longer communicate with the 90% who have been denied the opportunity to go to college.

But I hasten to add that I do not believe in the same kind of college for every one. I am not even sure that I believe in the kind of college we have today for the top 10% some call elite. And this kind of college, I think, is responsible for much of the campus revolt today. It simply does not, in my opinion, meet the requirements of our society, and is long overdue on an overhaul.

However, the antiqueness of our higher educational structure is only partially to blame for the growing impersonality in our colleges to which students object. The main blame must be placed on our college structure. If a university grows to 40,000 enrollments we insist upon handling them efficiently, above all. We introduce the ID number, bring in that symbol of system, the computer, set up lectures for 1200 at a time in auditoriums, where frequently students have to take notes in their laps. The professor, like a prima donna in an opera, or a conductor in a symphony, makes his grand entrances and exits three times a week without ever meeting a single student. If you don't think this happens listen to some freshmen discuss a psychology course with 1200 students in the class. And if this isn't bad enough all of these students had to scramble through a mob scene in the gymnasium registering for the course at the opening of the term. No wonder protesting students call this education by the numbers.

And the measure of it all is the classroom contact. In American higher education we prove that we are educated by something called a transcript. Like a bank book the transcript records the balance in credits and quality points. If a course meets three times a week for sixteen weeks you may expect to get three semester hours of credit. When you have accumulated the magic number of 124 you are entitled to collect your bachelor's degree.

It is the way these class credits have to be earned that has disaffected so many students. Despite the fact that the trend to college for all has introduced the widest range of individual differences ever before assembled in higher education, classes are held for a mythical average student. As a result, the gifted in the subject are unbearably bored; the underdeveloped discouragingly bewildered, and the students who comprise the bulge in the bell-shaped curve too often plod along uninspiredly. No wonder today's classroom is so often referred to as a lockstep.

That we have had a recent epidemic of demand for courses related to the study of Black peoples is not so much a manifestation of race consciousness as it is a revolt against the predatory disciplines. From a look at today's college curriculum one would have to conclude that Genesis should be rewritten in terms of our prescriptive disciplines. Every Monday, Wednesday and Friday, for example, at nine o'clock, the student studies chemistry. At eleven on the same days he turns his attention to Economics. And on Tuesday and Thursday at precisely ten o'clock, he may have a course in English literature. From the inviolability of the boundaries of these subjects it can only be assumed that on the First Day God was a chemist; on the second, an Economist; and on the third a dramatist. The nearest the student may come to an understanding of the unity of the universe is in three broad divisions labelled by some universities as sciences, social science, and humanities. That there is any relationship among them, or that there may be some other interests in the interstices are not provided for in the curriculum, despite its claim of liberal through some choices called electives or options

Well these are the three most frequent objections to education in general. What about education in the health sciences. If I appear to illustrate with medical education most often it is only because this major division of the health sciences education has most frequently come under protest in our media. Check my selection of the most frequently voiced criticisms of medical schools by medical students. Number one seems to be, to this layman, who once served as librarian of a medical school, "Get us to the patient sooner." Number two, get us into clinics earlier. Other criticisms seem to revolve around the rigidity of the curriculum, the antiquated learning mode.

There are, of course, many more dissatisfactions with medical education. Some of them seem to me quite ludicrous, if you will forgive me for expressing what is probably an unqualified opinion. I refer specifically to the recent request of the Dean in the School of Medicine, University of Colorado, to establish a clinic for hippies. They resent being made to wait in waiting rooms; asked intimate questions about their personal life. It is not from these noisy protesters, however, that any serious identifications of either problems or solutions can be expected.

As an educator, rather than as one qualified in the Health Sciences, the problems in medical education have been most thoughtfully stated in three contemporary sources. As a Fulbright Fellow in the United Kingdom some years ago I have developed a profound respect for our colleagues in Britain to think through maturely some of the professional unrest that confronts the world. This was certainly true in my own field of librarianship. Encouraged by my experiences in one profession I made inquiries among some of the medical librarians in England whom I know and respect. Brian Armitage, librarian of the Charing Cross Hospital Medical School Library, the University of London, put me on to several bits of reading.

Among these the report of the University of Nottingham's Medical School Advisory Committee appeared to sum up as they put it "three recent developments in medical education that have not favored the education of the doctor." First, they placed, "the increasing tendency to specialize." Next, they decried the increasing separation of medical students and staff from the rest of the university. Third, they pointed out, the medical man is older than ever before when he finally becomes independent, and that is bad because "new ideas and a sense of adventure are qualities of youth." You will be better able to judge the validity of these three points than I, but I cannot resist objecting to the last point, because my experience does not bear out a very high correlation between chronological age and intellectual adventuring.

A second contemporary statement on needed medical education change comes from the Harvard Medical School, on this side of the Atlantic. In the spring of 1967 seven members of the graduating class, fresh from their medical school experience put together a student "proposal for a new Harvard Medical School Curriculum." Writing in the *Harvard Medical Alumni Bulletin* under the title "A New Order of Things: The Impetus for Change in the Harvard Medical School Curriculum," one of the members of the class of '67 declared "the curriculum has again become unwieldy to the extent that it is in danger of failing to satisfy the objectives of comprehensive medical care . . ."

But not only the curriculum but the teaching, or what I call the learning mode, in medical schools fails to satisfy the objectives. "As students," writes this recent graduate of the Harvard Medical School, our first encounter with the medical school teacher is in the lecture hall . . . most agree that the systematic didactic lecture, to be effective, must be sparingly employed." Flexner, he quotes, said "good teachers accomplish most, not by painfully consuming their time and energy in over-elaboration that does everything for the student . . .", but rather in enabling the student to elaborate independently for himself.

I quote as my third source for a thoughtful criticism of medical education today an interview with Herbert Ratner, MD, director of public health for Oak Park, Illinois as recorded in the *Center Magazine*, published bimonthly by the Fund for the Republic, Inc., "I would say that most medical schools are confused about their basic purpose," says Dr. Ratner. "We do not know any longer whether our goal is to turn out physicians or research men . . . the true and chief function of the medical school (in Dr. Retner's opinion) is to turn out physicians, that is artists, not scientists; professional men, not high level technicians. We should appeal to students as humanitarians, not as technologists; as makers of health in the suffering rather than pursuers of truth in the laboratory . . ." These words from a practicing physician, from a city's health officer are at least ponderable.

In summary, it might be said that those who think rather than march, those who dialog rather than demonstrate, those in our academic communities who are more concerned about identifying solutions than about identifying problems, have focused their attention on three shortcomings of our education, general or in the health sciences: one, the growing impersonality caused by numbers now being educated; two, the learning mode, still dominated by the class contact and the lecture; three, the curriculum, which persists with predatory disciplines. But because these thoughtful critics, unlike the noisy minority who monopolize our media, these days, are earnestly concerned with solutions they are quietly but creatively experimenting and innovating with some dimentions that begin to describe prototypes for the education of tomorrow.

For instance, at Antioch College, in Yellow Springs, Ohio, where TVA engineer Arthur Morgan introduced into the institution founded by Horace Mann over a century before, at least two significant innovations—the work-study plan and autonomous courses—there has been established a center for experimental colleges. Twenty institutions of higher education are in this Union for experimentation. Under the leadership of Dr. Sam Baskin a number of significant experimentations with the learning mode have emerged. Most of these are concerned with variations on the theme of independent study by the student.

Several colleges and universities have begun to replace the classroom and the lecture as the dominant learning mode with periods of complete independent study. Florida Presbyterian College, for example, has a winter inter-term in January when all classes are suspended for a month so that students may study independently in the library. Emory University, which incidentally has a strong medical school, and work in the health sciences, established something called Wonderful Wednesday. On that day every week in all schools and departments there are no classes and students are urged to order their own learning mode.

Oklahoma Christian College, a denominational institution of the Church of Christ, considers a three semester hour course for example, a time contract between student and teacher which may result in three class meetings and six preparation hours some weeks; or nine preparation, independent study hours and no class meetings. Independent study at Oklahoma Christian, for example, is provided for by giving each student his own individual study carrel in the library, with considerable dial access to a variety of media.

The University of California at Santa Cruz, Pacific University, and Michigan State University are examples of institutions who are doing something experimentally about the problem of impersonality. Although Santa Cruz is authorized to go to 27,500 enrollment, eventually, cluster colleges are being established there, no one college will have as many as 1,000 students, thus insuring some educational intimacy. Pacific is made up of a number of small colleges, each with an academic accent, like Latin America, social sciences, natural sciences, humanities. Michigan State has made a start in converting a multiversity with all of the accoutrements of mass impersonality into something more intimate, by activating at least three prototype small colleges on campus. These colleges have been organized around dormitory centers.

And finally if you will look at the increasing number of conferences in education devoted to experimentation you will catch something of the optimistically creative spirit in our education that our television networks refuse to display as prominently as they do the coiffured gentry who march. Our own Florida State University, for example, sponsored a symposium on innovation at Wakulla Springs some years ago. There, eleven experimenting colleges and universities reported their new dimensions of higher education. You can read about them in a little book edited by Hugh Stickler titled *Experimental Colleges*. In Massachusetts, 40 experimenting colleges under a USOE grant and Union of Experimental College sponsorship reported some exciting innovations on these campuses.

One of these was the proposal for establishing a Library-College at Jamestown College in North Dakota. The previous December the President, some representatives of the administration, faculty and students of Jamestown College had met with some consultants and advocates of the Library-College idea to explore the application of the concept. The results of these explorations can be found in a volume published by the Drexel Press in 1966.

When a college is a library and a library is a college it is a Library-College. In a Library-College the basic learning mode is independent study by the student in the library under faculty guidance. From the Jamestown Charter I quote these words:

> ". . . the effectiveness of student learning, particularly through independent study with a bibliographically expert faculty."

About 100 experimenting colleges in the United States are now innovating with elements of the Library-College idea. Leaders in this educational movement have organized Library-College Associates, Inc., which publishes at the University of Oklahoma the quarterly *Library-College Journal,* and promotes periodic conferences, the next one to be held in the Lasalle Hotel, Chicago, in November.

Some have been good enough to credit the origin of the idea to me, but I acknowledge my debt to the 19th century English essayist Thomas Carlyle. In his book *Heroes and Hero Worship,* published about 1848, there is an essay entitled the *Hero as Man of Letters,* in which occur the often quoted words:

> *The True University these days is a collection of books.*

What is not quoted as often is the context from which these words are taken. It was Carlyle's contention that there is nothing a professor can do for his students but teach him how to read intelligently. Others have said the same thing in different words, among them my boyhood and continuing hero, the greatest teacher of physicians of this century, the late Sir William Osler. My admiration of Osler was responsible for my writing of an essay which has been reprinted many times in newspapers and in anthologies. I titled this essay "How to Find Time to Read." Osler was my chief model. Throughout his life he made it a rule to spend the last 15 minutes before retiring, no matter how early or how late at night, reading something besides his medical literature, and many of you will know how well read in medicine he was.

I quote from his magnificently inspired book, *A Way of Life,* in which he has a chapter on "The Student Life":

> "Divide your attention equally between books and men. The strength of the student of books is to sit still—two or three hours at a stretch—eating the heart out of a subject with pencil and notebook in hand, determined to master

> the details and intricacies, focusing all your energies on its difficulties. (p.178)

Here you have the spirit of independent study, the learning mode that is somehow washed away by the professor's tendency to pre-digest information for the student, to feed him like a baby with pablum. In his USOE pamphlet for the series *New Dimensions in Higher Education* Dr. Winslow Hatch declares that a measure of quality in education is the degree to which students can study independently. Well, the essence of the Library-College idea is to build educational self reliance in the student.

The idea is not new. Reading has been the heart of education not only in Britain but in the universities on the continent. I can recall that during my Fulbright year in the United Kingdom I never heard any one in the academic community speak of taking a course, or attending classes. Always the expression was "I am reading in Medicine"; I am reading in Chemistry; I am reading in European History; and of course, I am reading in English Literature, or in Philosophy.

Now, by reading, the Library-College does not mean reading only print. The dimension the Library-College has added to the Carlyle quote is an augmented understanding of what reading means. In the Library-College reading is done in what I have called the *Generic Book*. In my *Saturday Review* editorial I first defined the Generic Book as the sum total of man's communication possibilities. I came upon the definition and concept of the Generic Book, which formed the central theme in my subsequent book entitled *Instructional Materials,* through an anecdote.

On the mantel in our living room is a picture of me in World War II army uniform. Every time students come to visit us they look at the picture and ask, "Which war?" If I were sensitive about my age I could resent the implication of the question. As it is, I am frequently tempted not to disappoint them by answering Spanish American, if not War of 1812.

The fact is that although I was too young to fight in World War I, I have read a great deal about that war. In the course of my reading I came across this story. In war, as in no other human enterprise I know Death confronts us irresistibly. One moment you are talking to a buddy; the next moment he is gone. Troubled by this a French soldier once asked his General, My General, what is death?"

Spontaneously, the French general responded,
"Death? Why Death is sudden incommunicability."

Sudden incommunicability. No other definition has had quite the effect on me, and I have been interested in the subject of death for as long as I can remember. I have read much, including the recent symposium volume on "The Meaning of Death." It was my good fortune as a visiting professor at McGill to have met Dr. Francis, Sir William Osler's close associate, who showed me the copious notes Osler had always made on the moment when his patients passed from life to death. But in all of the literature on death that I have read no definition has influenced me quite as much as the French general's spontaneous declaration to the soldier.

Not only because it defined death. But really because it defined life. For if death is incommunicability, and that is what it is, because the dead person is no longer responding to you or to life, then life must be the opposite. Life must be communicability. And suddenly I understood that the only real evidence of life is communicability. And further I understood that the sum total of this communicability, all that man had ever communicated since the dawn of history was in all of the records, from the first pictography crudely drawn in the caves through modern television and computer assisted programmed media. The composite was the generic book, the sum total of man's communications through all of his five senses, and possibly through those mysterious extra senses we are just beginning to study in parapsychological laboratories at Duke, and Cambridge, and at the Sorbonne, and elsewhere.

This led to my classification of man's media by format, as well as by subject and level of maturity. Now the format of a medium is its physical makeup. What we have tended to call a book, almost exclusively, is the format that consists of printed pages bound in a hard cover of buckram, or fabrikoid, or cloth, or leather. But a paperback is also a book. And so, too, is a periodical, or a newspaper, or a pamphlet, or a government document. Before the invention of the printing press, books appeared almost exclusively in the format of manuscript, handwritten on papyrus, or parchment, with reed pens. After the invention of printing, books also began to appear as photographs, as motion pictures, as audial cylinders and discs, and later as tapes; as slides, and filmstrips, and transparency overlays; as radio and television; and as programmed responses on machines and computer consoles.

There are, of course, a few old fashioned librarians around who refer to anything but print as "non-book" materials. My students know that I am particularly allergic to this term. My favorite quote in this connection is from a 15th century librarian in a monastery who declared, "This is a real library. We have only books here (meaning manuscripts.) Here there are none of those non-book materials produced by a recently invented machine called a printing press." These words are still paraphrased by some unprogressive librarians with reference to so-called audiovisual media.

In all of the hullabaloo about Marshall McLuhan and the lack of understanding about what he is really saying, which Marshall McLuhan ingenuously admits himself, there is one very important principle he is reiterating. I tried to state it in my own book and shorter writings, unpsychedelically, of course, and that is fatal to any idea in our go-go age. The principle is simply that the format of a medium may affect its communicability in certain subject with different levels of maturity or receptivity. Translated into education it means that learning may be affected by the format of the medium. Some students may learn more effectively thru the medium format of print; others through television; still others through radio, or transparency overlays, or tapes, or programmed instructional media.

I apologize for this bit of abstraction. This philosophy is basic to an understanding of the learning mode in the Library-College. We contend that reading is more than reading a printed page. We believe reading means reading the generic book. As Frank Jennings has written in his thoughtful little book, *This Is Reading*:

> "But reading, remember, is not restricted to the printed page. Actually it never was . . . throughout his history man has "read" many things: the flight of birds, the guts of sheep, sun spots, liver spots, and the life lines on a hand. He has read the lore of the jungle, the spoor of the beast and the portents in a dish of tea . . ."

Let us then begin the description of the Library-College by identifying the first of its elements—the Learning Mode.

Basically, the Library-College student studies independently in the library by reading the generic book. He reads the printed page of course, but he also views visuals of all kinds, from flat pictures to slides, from 16mm motion pictures to videotapes; and he auds, (the technical term for listens) tapes and discs; radio and transcriptions. And he does all of this at what are now called "wet" carrels, with dial access to the whole range of formats that comprise the generic book. At Oklahoma Christian, for example, every student has his own, individual work bench, his carrel for which he pays a semester fee.

The students study under faculty bibliographic guidance. Not only is the new student more adept in the use of media; but so also is the new breed faculty, who now perform a new, sensitively artistic function in the learning process. The trend to college for all has presented us with the widest range of individual differences in students we have ever known. If it was possible to lecture with one lesson plan in the old days when only the upper 10% went to college, and the range of individual differences was narrower, it was certainly made necessary by the limited number of books available. Today, for the first time in the history of education we can match individual differences in students with individual differences in media.

But this really calls for a new breed faculty. It means we must now have professors who not only know their students' individual differences but the individual differences of media as well. And so the new breed faculty member becomes very much like the sensitive physician, a professional who can diagnose his student's individual capacity and preparation and prescribe the right media to educate. This does not mean there is no place for the lecture, or for the seminar, or for the class meeting. These, too are part of the generic book, but they are no longer all or most of it. They have their place as corollaries to the independent study by students bibliographically guided by the faculty.

Let us add one element in the Learning Mode which is advocated in what my colleagues call the Shores Library-College. For you must understand there are many variations on the idea. I have urged the "Each one Teach One" corollary, which has been made famous in the 20th century by the great missionary Dr. Laubach, in his world literacy effort. In the 18th century this idea was espoused by Bell and by Lancaster, and it was called the Monitorial method, under which each advanced student taught one beginning student. All of us who have taught know we have learned most about our subject in the first year by being forced to teach it to some one.

Interestingly enough, the Harvard medical students I referred to earlier as offering a proposal for a reformed medical education advocate the "each one teach one" method as a way to a better medical education. I quote:

> "The most effective way to insure that the medical student will cultivate good habits of independent thinking and scholarship . . . is to teach the medical student to teach."

Independent study by the student, plus each one teach one, under the bibliographic guidance of the faculty, with dialog, discussion, seminar and lecture broadly describe the learning mode of the Library-College. Does this suggest a learning mode for the Medical Library-College?

To accomplish this learning mode at least two other elements of the Library-College must be described. One is the curriculum; the other is the facility. On all levels of education the revolt is against predatory disciplines. The Library-College does not abandon the debt the older generation has to the new—to transmit the heritage so that each new generation may profit from the suc cesses and failures of the past. But the Library-College also believes that true dialog between the past and the present provides an opportunity for the new generation to contribute to curriculum development. It proposes, therefore, through something I call the student interest profile to find a place in the curriculum for the matter of greatest concern to the new generation as well.

I also propose to introduce two neglected areas. The first of these recognizes the truth of that quotation from the prolific writer Anon that adorns the arches of so many academic buildings:

The Half of Knowledge is Knowing Where to Find It.

If the Library, or the Media Center, or the Learning Resource Center, or any other name by which you wish to designate the Library of the Generic Book, is truly to be the center of the learning mode, then both faculty and students must have a greater media sophistication than they now have. I propose an augmented required course on media and library use, with accent on literature search know-how. All one has to do is watch some faculty, leave alone most students, work in libraries to realize what a poor job we who claim to be librarians have done over the years.

The other neglected area, for want of a title, I merely call *Knowledge*. It attempts to relate the sciences and the humanities, and erase the artificial boundary between the two cultures that C. P. Snow set up in his much cited essay. Further, this area would attempt to fill in the interstices among the predatory disciplines. It might even stimulate in both students and faculty a bit of serendipity, a term which the sciences have but recently rediscovered.

The second element which must be described is the facility. I understand you are now considering facilities for an ultimate student body of some 5,000. As you plan your library or media center take into account the trend toward independent study; the inevitable approach to the Library-College concept. This means some radical revision of previous library architecture requirements.

In planning a library, three basic accomodations must be considered: one, accommodations for students; two, accommodations for stock; three, accommodations for faculty and staff. Previously our standards for student accommodation suggested that 25-30% of the total student body should be seated in the library. This is moving steadily upward toward 100% as the trend to independent study accelerates and enrollments mount. Oklahoma Christian provides 110%. If you are going to 5,000 students then you should consider the cluster college idea, with no one college exceeding 1,000 students, and the individual college libraries providing 100% seating. Furthermore this seating should take the form of carrels, wired for dial access.

Stock accommodation, previously planned to shelve hard cover print, primarily, with after thought provisions for storing periodicals, newspapers, maps, and, occasionally discs, but never films, and other audiovisuals and their equipment, must now from the start consider the housing of every format of the generic book. Furthermore, it must increasingly include some kind of an electronic core for dial access and remote computer consoles.

Staff accommodation must account for more than the clerical and paraprofessional housekeepers of the past, plus their professsional supervisors. Under the independent study learning mode it is essential that faculty offices be placed in the library. Furthermore, seminars, conference rooms, classrooms, and lecture halls, in close proximity are paramount. Nor must previewing and pre-auding rooms be neglected.

Well, there you have in broad outline the concept of the Library-College as it now confronts American higher education with some solutions. You who are involved in Health Sciences Education will be in a better position to translate the dimension into a Medical Library-College.

I believe in the Library-College idea. I believe in it because it contains answers to many of the legitimate problems intellectual critics of our American education are advancing. I submit to you, my peers in education, the bases for a Medical Library-College. May your efforts and mine for educational reform result in prototypes for tomorrow's better higher education of America.

REFERENCES

1. Hippocratic Oath. *Collier's Encyclopedia.* 1969. v.12. p.136.
2. Shores, Louis. "Preprofessional Education of Librarians. (In University of Chicago, Education for Librarianship; ed. by Bernard Berelson. A.L.A., 1949. p. 109-14)
3. University of Nottingham. Report of the Medical School Advisory Committee. June, 1965. 76p.
4. Wesley, J. R. "A New Order of Things: The impetus for change in the Harvard Medical School Curriculum." *Harvard Medical Alumni Bulletin.* Spring, 1968. p.4-10.
5. Flexner, Abraham. *Medical Education.* 1925.
6. Ratner, Herbert (Interviewed by Donald McDonald. "Second Edition of Medicine in America." *The Center Magazine.* May 1969. v.2, p.19-26.
7. Union for Experimental Colleges. *Brochure.* Yellow Springs, Ohio, 1969.
8. Bevan, John. "The Inter-Term at Florida Presbyterian College." *Library-College Journal,* Summer, 1969. v.2.
9. Emory University. "Wonderful Wednesday." Atlanta, Ga., 1969.
10. North, Stafford. "The Sound of Learning at Oklahoma Christian College." Oklahoma City, 1965.
11. Stickler, W. H. Experimental Colleges, Tallahassee, Florida State University, 1965.
12. U.S.O.E. Innovation in Higher Education; a conference held at Magnolia, Mass., 1966.
13. Shores, Louis, *et al. The Library-College.* Philadelphia, Drexel Press, 1966.
14. Carlyle, Thomas. *Heroes and Hero Worship.* 1848.
15. Shores, Louis. "How To Find Time To Read." *Omnibook,* May 1953. v.15, p. 121-23.
16. Osler, Sir William. *A Way of Life.* Dover Publications, Inc., 1951. 278p.
17. Hatch, Winslow. New Dimensions in Higher Education. Washington, D.C., U.S.O.E., 1965.

18. Shores, Louis. "Books: Continuous Communicability." *Saturday Review*, March 22, 1958. v.41, p.26.
19. Shores, Louis *Instructional Materials*. Ronald, 1960. Chapter 1.
20. *The Vespasiano Memoirs*. (Lives of Illustrious Men of the XVth Century); by Vespasiano Da Bisticci. N.Y., Lincoln Mac Veegh.
21. McLuhan, Marshall. *Understanding Media*. 1965.
22. Jennings, Frank G. *This Is Reading*. N.Y., Teachers College, Columbia University, 1965.
23. Wesley, *op. cit.* p. 10.

LIBRARY-COLLEGE USA

PART FOUR: LIBRARY-COLLEGE FOUNDATIONS

17.

THE LIBRARY ARTS COLLEGE, A POSSIBILITY IN 1954?[1]

(The original essay for the American Library Association World's Fair Convention, Chicago, 1934. First published in *School and Society*, 1965, 41:110-14)

THE SPONSOR of any untried plan, no matter how worth while, faces at the outset two discouraging types of criticism. There are first those reactionary critics who defend the *status quo* by hurling charges of charlatanism or radicalism at any proponent of change, without pretending to examine the proposal itself. And then, there are those who will listen kindly and tolerantly to the presentation of a reform, and at the conclusion dismiss it as Utopian and fanciful.

To the first group of critics the sponsor of the present plan can merely say solemnly and with all the sincerity at his command that he honestly believes the changes he proposes are vital to the education of young men and women and therefore important to society. It is somewhat easier to tell the second group of critics that the library arts college idea is not new, that it has been predicted for over a half century and that trends in current college reform point inevitably to the consummation of the plan, possibly before the assigned 1954 date.

Every librarian has used the Carlyle quotation, "The true University is a collection of books." That pioneer historian of pedagogy, Gabriel Compayré, commenting on Abelard's ability as a lecturer, prophesied the downfall of classroom methods over a half century ago, when he wrote in his epochal work:

> Human speech, the living word of the teacher, had then an authority, an importance, which it has lost in part *since books, everywhere distributed, have, to a certain extent, superseded oral instruction.* At a time when printing did not exist, when manuscript copies were rare, a teacher who combined knowledge with the gift of speech was a phenomenon of incomparable interest. . . .[2]

How much more strongly Monsieur Compayré would have stated this thought had he lived to witness the replacement of the single-textbook method by the modern reserve book system can only be surmised.

If time permitted, a series of statements by educators and librarians culled from writings and speeches of the last half century and arranged chronologically could be presented here to support the contention that the education of the future will inevitably be a library education, that is, an education which will be centered in the library. A few such quotations may suffice. For example, in the National Education Association proceedings of 1889, the U.S. Commissioner of Education, W. T. Harris, was quoted as declaring, "The school is set at the task of teaching the pupil how to use the library in the best manner—that, I take it, *is the central object toward which our American schools have been unconsciously tending.*"[3]

The president-elect of the American Library Association quoted President Harper, of the University of Chicago, as follows:

> That factor of our college and university work, the library, fifty years ago almost unknown, today already the center of the institutional intellectual activity, half a century hence, with its sister, the laboratory, . . . *will by absorbing all else have become the institution itself.*[4]

Nor have these remarks come from educationists alone. In 1916, Librarian Richardson made a startling substitution for Mark Hopkins on his end of the log when he declared:

> It is conceivable that a university should be a university, and a student get a university education if the university consisted only of a library and a student, without a lecturer, tutor, or preceptor, or *research professor,* or librarian—absolutely only a student and a library on a desert island.[5]

We pass by the hosts of criticisms directed against the American college during the two decades following Librarian Richardson's observation, omitting such readable if not absolutely accurate books as Upton Sinclair's *Goose-Step* and Abraham Flexner's *Universities,* for the words of a college professor and a college student.

The professor is Carter Davidson writing on the "University of the Future":

> The faculty and the better students find the lecture and classroom recitation repetitious, boring, and a waste of time; the inferior students feel that lectures are hard to understand, and that classroom recitations are too rapid, failing to make clear the more difficult problems.[6]

The student is Kenneth Roberts' University of Michigan composite who when asked if he could suggest a remedy for the lack of scholarship in the "lit" school shot back:

> I certainly can! I came here to study. If somebody'd tell me what to study, I could do more by myself, in my own room and in a library, than I could by tramping around to a lot of lectures. . . . I don't get much of anything out of classes. . . .[7]

If these few quotations appear to deal harshly with the conventional college and the sacred faculty college, librarians humbly serve, look at what current reform has done to American higher education. The 31st yearbook of the National Society for the Study of Education lists 128 reforms which differ only in the degree of instructional responsibility placed on the library. Whether the innovation is styled honors reading, as at Swarthmore, or autonomous courses, as at Antioch; whether the teacher appointed to instruct is called tutor, as at Harvard, or preceptor, as at Princeton, or even professor of books, as at Rollins; whether courses are abolished, as at Chicago or Olivet, and comprehensive examinations instituted, the educational department fundamentally affected is the college library. Current college reformers have at last begun to realize that the material unit of cultural education is the book, and that actually, as well as oratorically, the library is the liberal arts' laboratory. Only the conception of the library as the college and the college as the library remains prerequisite to the birth of the library arts college.

Just how do these trends affect us as college librarians? In the first place, I should like to make a distinction between educational librarianship on the one hand and research librarianship on the other. This is fundamental, because I believe the two (education and research) are as incompatible in the library as they are in education.

The notion is rapidly gaining ground in college circles that a good researcher is not necessarily a good teacher. Indeed, there are those courageous enough to declare positively that the instructor engaged in research is invariably a poor teacher. No small part of the blame for the inferiority of undergraduate instruction can be traced to the fact that every American college is anxious to become a university engaged in research. The college president is forever exhorting his faculty to produce because he knows he can interest foundations in studies much more easily than he can in that intangible something called "good teaching." As a result, the college neglects its real job—the training of young men and women. If the truth were told, a high positive correlation would be found to exist between the amount of time and energy expended by the college faculty on research and the amount of time and energy devoted by the students to extracurricular activities. Mutually bored by the learning process as carried on in the classroom, the instructor seeks fame and advancement through research, and the student left to his own resources, endeavors to while away the four years as pleasurably as possible in the fraternity houses and stadia.

It is not the purpose of this paper to disparage the recent movement to create research librarianships. So long as American universities continue to produce tons of studies, useful and otherwise, each year, there will be need for research libraries and their staffs, whose duties will include the acquisition and organization of printed material *ad infinitum,* and the provision of even larger quarters for their accommodation.

Far different is the function of the educational library, such as the average undergraduate college should have. Its collection should be highly selective and definitely limited in size and scope. Whereas the research library's book selection problem may be solely one of acquisition, the educational library will be equally concerned with elimination. As protection against the nuisance of research ambitions, the college collection should have a maximum, say 35,000 volumes, imposed upon it, beyond which its collection may *never* expand. Each year the college may undertake to purchase 500 new titles, on condition it weed ont 500 old works from its collection for discard or for presentation to some ambitious research university endeavoring each year to report a bigger and better library. In this way only the number will remain static; the educational library's contents will always include the basic books, plus an ever-changing collection of ephemeral material. The result will be a highly serviceable educational library with abundant material to furnish a true culture to young people who want it. Another result of this selectivity will be to eliminate the necessity for providing expansion in college library buildings. Contrary to the Carnegie standard, I see no reason for planning future expansion in a college library building, if those responsible for book selection do a full job.

With the collection definitely limited in size and the actual titles standardized by some such basic list as the Shaw list, the acquisition and organizational duties in the college library will be reduced considerably and rendered largely routine. For example, it is entirely likely that college titles will be purchasable completely classified and cataloged, or that perhaps the H. W. Wilson Company will issue book catalogs cumulatively in which each college will be able to indicate its own holdings. In any event, it is very unlikely that the services of a highly trained cataloger and classifier will ever be needed in an educational library.

The question then arises what, if any, will be the librarian's duties? Primarily, the professional librarian will be instructor. The positions of librarian and professor will merge. Every college instructor will be library trained; every college librarian will be either a professional instructor in some field or a semi-professional housekeeper performing the necessary routines accessory to library education.

With this preliminary interpretation of higher educational trends, it is now possible to look at the library arts college of 1954. A somewhat more detailed description of the plan has been placed in Professor Phelps' hands, and no doubt his comments will elaborate the bare outline given here. The plan resulted from the writer's undergraduate experiences, which, like those of many other college students, convinced him he could learn much more in the library reading than he could by attending most classes. Since then, the plan has gradually developed an ambition to undertake undergraduate instruction to a small group of college men with a selected book collection of not over 1,000 titles, three library-trained instructors, and a small amount of equipment.

At the outset it should be realized that the library arts college is merely the logical culmination of such current trends in American higher education as are exemplified by honors courses, comprehensive examinations and other reforms of the last decade. Unencumbered by outworn appendages, the library arts college benefits from advantages minimized by the transitory experiments of today. It differs from the conventional college in at least five essentials.

In the first place, the library arts college reverses the conventional college's practice of compulsory, regular class attendance supplemented by voluntary and irregular library reading. The library arts college student is definitely scheduled for supervised reading periods and permitted to ask for a class meeting whenever he feels his readings have failed to answer questions. The supervisor of the reading period is a library trained subject-matter instructor. When the student reports to the history reading room for his history reading period, he finds there a history instructor thoroughly trained in library methods, who, among other things, combines the duties of the history instructor and the reference librarian.

In the second place, all instructional quarters, like classrooms, reading rooms and laboratories, are concentrated in the campus' one educational building—the library. A plan for such a building drawn to scale is available among my notes for anyone who cares to examine it. In general, the drawing calls for four units, one for each of the three subject divisions—humanities, natural sciences, social sciences—and a fourth for administrative and general reading quarters.

In the third place, the instructional scheme employs a principle of the Lancasterian schools which influenced American educational development in the early years of the nineteenth century, and which disappeared only because of improper conditions. Briefly, the principle calls for upper-class students to tutor lower-class students. This practice is mutually beneficial since it insures individual instruction for each lower classman and excellent training for each upper classman. Beginning teachers frequently attest they learned more about their major subject the first year they taught it than they learned in all their undergraduate study. Obviously, when a student has to know his lesson well enough to make it clear to an underclassman, that student not only masters his material, but what is more important, he is able to express himself clearly on the subject. This type of tutoring, reinforced by faculty supervision, supplemented by occasional inspirational lectures, and checked by the requirement of frequent papers, tests and a final comprehensive examination, will do much to restore scholarship to its rightful place on the college campus.

As for the faculty members themselves, they will be library-trained, subject-matter experts, but not specialists in the restricted sense which describes our present research professors who teach only incidentally. The chemistry man, for example, will not be so thoroughly consumed by his interest in colloids that he will be unable to supervise a general reading course in science. It is very likely that he will be able to express an intelligent opinion on James Joyce or the Herbartian influence in American education. But above all, he will be vitally interested in the young people he teaches, study their development as zealously as the average researcher does his experiment, and be as proud of the young man or woman he graduates into society as the average scientist is about a notable discovery.

Finally, the curriculum, instead of including a great number of frequently unrelated courses, will represent a carefully planned reading program intended to acquaint the student with man's accomplishments of the past and problems of the present. There is no more direct method of achieving this end than through reading the right books. To the library-trained instructor of the future is assigned the task of selecting intelligently the right book for the right student at the right time. That American Library Association motto might well be adopted as the major aim of library arts college education.

REFERENCES

1. Reprinted from *School and Society*, Vol. XLI (January 26, 1935), pp. 110-114, first delivered at the Chicago Century of Progress Exposition, 1934.
2. Gabriel Compayré, *The History of Pedagogy*. Boston: D. C. Heath & Co., 1901, p. 75.
3. N. E. A., Addresses and proceedings. Washington, National Education Association, 1889, p. 26.
4. Charles H. Compton, "The Library in Relation to the University," *Library Journal*, Vol. 35 (November, 1910), p. 503.

5. E. C. Richardson, "The Place of the Library in a University," *A. L. A. Bulletin*, Vol. 10 (January, 1916), p .8.
6. Carter Davidson, "University of the Future," *North American Review*, Vol. 231 (March, 1931), p. 531.
7. Kenneth Roberts, "Murmuring Michigan," *Saturday Evening Post*, Vol. 206 (1934), pp. 82-83.

18.

THE SHORES LIBRARY-COLLEGE: AN OUTLINE[1]

(Outline-essay prepared for the Jamestown College Library-College Conference, December, 1965.)

LEARNING MODE

I. *"Passing" of the classroom as a mode of learning.*

L. C. (Library-College) reverses present relationship between library and classroom. Instead of a *class meeting* in U. S. History on Monday, Wednesday, and Friday from 9-10 A.M. and *Library Reading* when the student can get to it, L. C. schedules *Library Reading in U. S. History,* Monday, Wednesday, Friday from 10-12 and class meeting when the students feel the need for one, or not at all if individual conference, small seminar, inspired lecture is preferred.

II. *Library Reading.*

This is the learning mode. Tough, hard struggle with the printed word is the regimen. Education is a struggle. Suffering is a prelude to learning. This is not to say medicine must be bitter to be good. On the contrary, "creative understanding" affords a sweet triumph. Library Reading underwrites *viability.* But is does much more than provide power to maintain existence; it arms the young mind to contend with the riddle of

1. This outline and miniature essay is based on a book-length manuscript currently being written titled *U.S.A. (United States University)*;*Idea for an American University,* which includes a cluster of Library-Colleges.

the universe, to ask "Who am I?", "Why should I exist at all?", "Is there any point to maintaining existence, to viability?".

III. *Library Viewing, Auding, Tasting, Smelling, Feeling are also part of the learning mode.*

And for that reason the L. C. library includes all formats. Each format has a peculiar pertinence to the individual learning situation occurring at various points in the student's college life. The unique strengths and weaknesses of each of the 100 or more classes of educational media, from textbook through television including programmed, manual and computerized devices should be part of the equipment used by the new generation of college faculty, a cross between the best qualities for the present classroom instructor and librarian-teacher.

IV. *"Each One Teach One."*

Under this system, as they advance in their work students become, under faculty direction, instructors, tutors, or monitors of students not as far along. This method provides a natural complement for the Library Learning Mode, benefiting not only the student but the tutor. All of us learned more about our subject by teaching it.

CURRICULUM

Generalia Areas

Reading Area A   Information Retrieval
Reading Area B   Knowledge

Knowledge

Reading Area C   Humanities
Reading Area D   Social Sciences
Reading Area E   Sciences
Reading Area F   Physical Culture
Reading Area G   Useful Arts

Specialty Units

Reading Unit   C1   Philosophy
               C2   Religion

	C3	Music
	C4	Visual Art
	C5	Language-Literature
Reading Unit	D1	Sociology
	D2	Political Science
	D3	Economics
	D4	Anthropology
	D5	Psychology
Reading Unit	E1	Mathematics
	E2	Astronomy-Space
	E3	Physics
	E4	Chemistry
	E5	Biology (Life Sciences)
Activity Unit	F1	Athletics
	F2	Dance
	F3	Self-Defense
	F4	Gymnastics
	F5	Swimming
Activity Unit	G1	Agriculture
	G2	Health
	G3	Food
	G4	Clothing
	G5	Shelter
	G6	Etiquette
	G7	Marriage and the Family

V. *"The Half of Knowledge is Knowing Where to Find It."*

Current Freshman orientation in library use, whether a half-hour "Cook's tour" during the opening days, a one-semester hour separate course, or a six-clock hour unit in Freshman English, is at best only a beginning. Ignorance of basic reference books, the components of this "half," is daily demonstrated by the inept hadling of these tools. For 105 years, *Statesman's Yearbook* has appeared annually with the most compact and authoritative data on the governments of the world. Yet, even majors and faculty in government neglect this source. *Information Retrieval* earns a curriculum place, therefore, that it has never had before.

VI. *"The Other Half"* is much more *inter*-disciplinary than subject areas. It is now "old hat" to point to an "integrated" curriculum that consists of "phy sci" in place of separate courses in chemistry, physics, geology; humanities in place of isolated offerings in philosophy, literature, and music. The time has come for beginning and capstone syntheses. Along with the generalist *Information Retrieval* offering must come a "generalia" course in knowledge which interrelates science, social science and humanities and confirms the unity of the universe.

VII. *The Five Major Areas* complement the two generalia and are somewhat like the components of post-World War II general education. Each reading area consists of Reading Units which resemble and provide a transition from present courses. But the word "reading" is emphasized, based on the precedent in England where a student "reads" in history, philosophy, physics, and even mathematics. It is further confirmation that evaluating a student's achievement shall not be measured in terms of class contacts.

Areas C, D, E comprise five reading units designated by subjects which currently name our academic departments. They are areas in which reading (including auding, viewing, and other sensory and extra-sensory media of communication) predominates, and in which activities (principally laboratory, field trip) are secondary. However, performance (writing and oral) is considerable.

Areas F and G are predominantly activity and performance; reading is enlisted but is secondary. These areas aim to prepare men to *do,* just as Area A-E aims to prepare students to *think, know, feel, appreciate,* and *believe.*

Self-defense is a vital part of every boy's and girl's life. Instruction and practice in boxing, wrestling, judo and other aspects of the manly art deserve a place. The dance as an art or as a social grace is in demand. Inter-collegiate football deserves a place not only as a more colorful spectacle than the late Ernest Hemingway's bull fight, but as a much more creative release of those forces which promote demonstration and rebellion in less mature nations. There is educational, esthetic, ethical and physical development in playing games to win according to well defined rules. All of the current collegiate sports including circus should be encouraged.

Area G is intended to equip every college graduate to assume responsibilities in home and community. It includes handyman skills for the man and homemaking proficiency for the woman. The range of units comprehends such prosaic but necessary talents as fixing leaking faucets, repairing torn screens, painting neglected exteriors, preparing balanced and delectable meals, knitting, sewing, child care, first aid, gardening, and etiquette.

Overall, the curriculum is a continuous interplay between the broad general and the minute special with all the degrees in between. A student's broad reading, at first, and concurrently later, in the two "Generalia" and five "Knowledge" areas leads to increasing concentrations in specialist units and specialized topics. As he approaches the senior months he is recalled by the "capstone" period in his knowledge area which seeks to interrelate the many particles with which he has been concerned.

STUDENTS

The Jamestown College Catalog statement of interest in "extending admission consideration to academically capable students of good character, emotional stability, high morale, and seriousness of purpose" is fundamental. The particular interest in "those who demonstrate special abilities in extra-curricular areas" adds a bit of insurance for a well-rounded student community. Especially comforting is the absence of the vindictive and often flaunting declaration of interest "only in the superior student." Such colleges are cowards. Nor should an independent study, library-centered college be for the "superior student" only. Rather, I believe the "class contact" college has been even more difficult for the "average" than for the "superior" student, and impossible for the below average student. Consequently, a heterogeneous student body is recommended for the L. C.: all ranges of intellectual ability, skill, talent, physical perfection, wide representation geographically, including people from other nations and non-Christian faiths.

Only the limitations of the Jamestown statement are desirable. To evaluate, the standard tests and secondary school performance, letters of reference and interview, health certification, and comment from a religious affiliation should be included in the admission folder.

Quantitatively, 400 to 800 students should constitute one L. C. As the upper figure is approached a second L. C. should be activated and then a third, so no matter how large the campus, impersonality is prevented by this organizational cluster of small colleges, Oxford, Cambridge—like.

FACULTY

Ultimately the new breed will be a cross of the best found among those who today teach predominately by classroom lecture, discussion-recitation, and those who guide through library reading, auding, viewing.

Presently there are enough classroom instructors and library counsellors in both ranks (classroom and library) to provide a nucleus faculty for the L. C. There are also some graduate students who because they are less committed to the classroom contact "lock-step" can be more easily re-oriented. Under this direction, student monitors, tutors, fellows will herald the next generation of college faculty.

LIBRARY

For an undergraduate L. C. 20,000 titles are basic. This will represent many more volumes and items.

Oualitatively, the parts of the selection are (1) Reference (basic lists); (2) General Reading (books every educated man should read) The *Harvard Classics, The Great Books* and by innumerable other lists; (3) *Hard Cover and Paperback Books* (divided by faculty decision with such assistance as library aids and reviews offer); (4) *Serials,* including a selection of newspapers, periodicals, scholarly journals, government publications; (5) *Graphics* largely library and faculty produced instructional materials; (6) *Projections* (still, opaque and transparent, motion, micro); (7) *Transmission* (disc, tape, radio, tv, computer); (8) *Programmed,* media, manual, mechanical, electronic; (9) *Community resources* (compilations, guides, contacts, reports relating to natural, institutional, human resources).

Library organization should take advantage of central technical processing wherever possible to release librarian-teachers from housekeeping duties. Broad classification, preferably by D. C. third summary in most instances, because of that system's greater mnemonic and instructional potential, and now with the 17th edition more up-to-date than Library of Congress. However, if the latter is adopted, copy classification exactly, without tampering.

Plan for print-out book catalogs instead of central card catalog. Provide copies of total catalog for all faculty regularly kept up-to-date by computerized supplements and cumulations.

FACILITY

Since the Library is the College, academically, it is the main building of every campus. Thus a university consists of a cluster of Library-Colleges, somewhat after the Cambridge, Oxford pattern and reflected in U. S. trends at Santa Cruz, Pacific, Michigan State, and elsewhere.

The Library-College may be planned as a quadrangle—with four major building units: (1) Library-College; (2) Dormitory and recreation; (3) Laboratory, shop, gymnasium, for activity, performance; (4) Chapel for meditation, worship, quiet forces of music, art.

The Library-College building may be octagonal or circular. At the core is a traditional (not a modular) stack, two to eight tiers high to correlate with circumference reading—study-conference of one to four stories high. Circumference areas will relate with the Dewey stack segments approximately.

Curriculum Area	*Dewey*
A & B	000-099.
C	100-149; 179-199; 200-299; 390-399; 400-499; 700-789; 800-899; 920-29.
D	300-389; 900-919; 930-999.
E	500-599.
F	790-799.
G	600-699.

Reader accommodation is 100%, individual carrel or station. Table accommodations are available in conference rooms, seminars, near index, catalog, viewing, auding, and certain other group facilities. Carrels are located in the inner circumference contiguous with stacks. Faculty office-studies, large enough for faculty research, preparation, and conference with up to three persons at one time are located in the inner-outer circumference along with work rooms. Seminars, listening and viewing rooms, each accommodating 10 to 20 are located in the outer circumference.

Lighting, darkening, acoustics, outlets provide for newer media including "listening posts" in reading areas and eschew modular construction for the L. C. building. Campus lawn esthetically landscaped and possibly a center fountain. Outside of central area place the athletic fields and "where the action is" equipment.

FINANCE

Parsons College has shown the way to independence. Many parents share the quest for a college opportunity for young people. If a $2,000 to $3,000 annual cost for college is now within the pocketbook of the nation then a 500-student college underwrites, independently, a million to a million and a half dollar program. This should cover food, shelter, recreation, health protection and academics.

Approximately (for 500 students)

Food	250,000
Housing	$100,000
Health, recreation, etc.	50,000
Library materials and maintenance (clerical)	50,000
Faculty salaries	
Distinguished visiting lecturers (20 @ $1,000)	20,000
Distinguished resident scholars (5 @ $20,000)	100,000
Library Professors (40 @ average $8,000)	320,000
Administration	100,000
Contingent	210,000

EVALUATION

Most difficult of all is the measure of education, for the L. C. evaluation must be eclectic in the transition period utilizing all conventional instruments and devices for the sake of comparability and transfer. Qualitatively, writing, speaking, performing tests must be utilized. In preparation for these, students undertake:

Writing of weekly, term, comprehensive essays, quizzes, examinations. Standardized tests are used wherever possible with stimulation to achieve without apology, for best national averages, for preeminence.

Speaking, dialogue, debate, forum, tape, assembly, at scheduled, frequent opportunities.

Oral examinations of both information finding and concept exposition. For the former, a type of competitive "college bowl" or tournament device should be constructed. Despite criticism of the "walking encyclopedia" kind of learning, L. C. can demonstrate that it is more effective even in this kind of learning And since most national tests are heavily slanted in this direction, L. C. cannot afford to disdain.

Performing should strive not only for excellence but for record breaking. Perhaps the Russian method of keeping constantly in front of their athletes existing performance records in their specialties has advantages over Big Ten Conference restraints against winning.

19.

LIBRARY-COLLEGE CHARTER

(The Charter was written by a committee of the Jamestown College conference on the Library-College, December, 1965, of which committee B. Lamar Johnson was chairman, and Louis Shores a co-writer member.)

THE PURPOSE of the Library-College is to increase the effectiveness of student learning, particularly through (though not limited to) the use of library-centered, independent study with a bibliographically expert faculty. This charter assumes that the "Library-College concept" can and should be adapted to colleges with varying objectives and philosophies. The curriculum of a particular Library-College must emerge from its objectives and philosophy.

I. Library centered, independent study with a bibliographically expert faculty requires:

   A. Library materials: As conceived in this statement, library materials represent varying viewpoints and typically include the following organized for independent use:
      1. Reference sources representing knowledge in all pertinent fields.
      2. The Good Books (basic editions of the great monuments of human thought—the time-tested classics).
      3. Representation of the better current literature in all pertinent fields, including hard covers, paper-backs, serials, etc.
      4. Graphics (maps, globes, charts, pictures, dioramas, realia, etc.).

5. Projections (transparencies, slides, film strips, microfilms).
6. Transmissions (disc, tape, radio, TV).
7. Resources (human, social, natural).
8. Mechanical, automated, electronic, computer, programmed and other "new educational media."

B. Independent study: With faculty assistance it will typically include:
1. Definition of goal or problem.
2. Selection of methods of study or investigation.
3. Conduct of study or investigation.
4. Report of findings.
5. Evaluation of findings.

C. Bibliographically expert faculty: The faculty will be expert in knowing:
1. Library materials as defined in A above in their respective fields.
2. How to use library materials as defined in A above as vehicles of learning in their respective fields.

D. Students at Library-College: Students will be expected to achieve competence:
1. In reading, writing, speaking, and listening.
2. In critically using resources of learning (including library materials defined in A above) in independent study and investigation.
3. In intelligently relating these resources to the educational objectives and philosophy of the particular college in which they are enrolled.

II. Library-centered, independent study, with a bibliographically expert faculty will typically—though not invariably—require:

A. Abundance of appropriate materials as defined in IA above.
B. Merging of present library and classroom teaching functions in the same individual—the new breed faculty member.
C. Library facilities which appropriately permeate the campus.

D. Varied syllabi, bibliographies, and reading guides.
E. Abundance of activity related to varying views on controversial ideas and issues.
F. Cooperative exploration, discovery, and synthesis by faculty and students rather than perpetuating a "master-disciple" relationship.

III. Since life is broader than library-centered independent study students will have planned experience in other and varied aspects of living. To this end library resources will be used as much as possible to enrich such activities as the following to be selected on the basis of the objectives and philosophy of a given college:

A. Worship and meditation.
B. Participation in the fine arts.
C. Conducting scientific and other experiments.
D. Participation in discussions, forums, and lectures.
E. Participation in citizenship and community service.
F. Participation in the practical arts.
G. Participation in recreation and social activities.
H. Engaging in field work.

20.

The purpose of the Library-College is to increase the effectiveness of student learning particularly through the use of the library-centered independent study with a bibliographically expert faculty. (from the Jamestown Charter)

ANOTHER PREFACE

(The Preface to the book *The Library-College,* edited by Louis Shores, Robert Jordan, and John Harvey, and published by Drexel Press in 1966, was written by Louis Shores and co-signed.)

EXPERIMENTING COLLEGES are preparing the United States for another historical first—the higher education of all the people. As millions of students pour out of our high schools in search of learning, post-secondary institutions struggle with several urgent quandaries: the impersonality of numbers; the wider range of individual differences; the accelerated torrent of information; the unlimited commitment to specialization; and perhaps problems which others would measure more threatening. Current experiments deal with all of these aspects of higher learning.

To contend with the inevitable numbers several of our so-called "multiversities" with student populations approaching 100,000 are taking a cue from the British university and reorganizing into small, personal colleges. To match the range of individual differences in young people a wide range of learning resources is being acquired, organized and disseminated by the library. To counter a zealous, national worship of the specialist many colleges are offering "integrated" or "inter-disciplinary" programs encompassing broad segments of knowledge.

INDEPENDENT STUDY

For the student, these new programs are characterized by independence from the lock-step pre-digested oral informing in average measured doses. Labelled in experimenting colleges variously as honors reading, autonomous courses, tutorial instruction, preceptorial teaching or just independent study, the central theme is that each student is a unique individual who works best at his own pace toward his own objective at an individual "work bench" in the library. The instructors are bibliographically competent counsellors available for individual counselling, for group discussions and for periodic lectures that provide elements not available in print or other formats.

The logical conclusion of this trend toward independent study is the Library-College. Several of the experimenting colleges today approach this conception. Over the years Antioch has hovered over the idea. At Stephens for years the Dean and the Librarian were the same person; today, an advanced library-instructional complex reveals the potential for learning in all formats from textbooks through television. Monteith at Wayne State has demonstrated a new relationship between those who teach in the classroom and those who teach in the library. Florida Presbyterian dismisses all classes in January so the students may concentrate in the library.

And now a Library-College is about to be born. From December 17 to 21, 1965, 30 exponents of the Idea gathered at Jamestown College, Jamestown, North Dakota, to design a Library-College for that campus. Led by Dan Sillers, a President with vision and courage, and, above all, a talent for working with faculty and students, an uplifting experience occurred. For many of the participants, it was the best conference they had ever experienced; for others, it was a turning point in their lives. From early morning until late at night people talked, read, designed, displayed elements of the new college for challenge, revision, remolding. Some of these components are on display in Part III.

In preparation for the Jamestown meeting each participant was invited to describe an ideal Library-College or any of its components, and these essays are offered as Part II.

Those who accepted this invitation had been brought up on a developing pre-Library-College literature going back at least to the often-quoted but frequently under-estimated Carlyle statement from his essay on the *Hero as Intellectual*: "The True University is a Collection of Books." Representative parts of that literature comprise Part I.

Therefore, this collection of essays, papers, committee reports, and appendices is offered to college and university presidents, to classroom and library faculties, to public and private supporters of higher education, to students pre, in, and post-college as a prediction of things to come in the nation first to commit itself to universal *higher* education.

The present book is an anthology of various kinds of papers concerning the Library-College idea and covers many different facets of it. The reader may be concerned about some repetition of ideas among the papers included here. Obviously similar ideas have occurred to several leaders in librarianship and higher education at different times and this should give added impact to their importance.

In sharing the task of preparing the volume for publication Louis Shores and Robert Jordan have compiled and edited its contents from Workshop contributions, while John Harvey did final revision and editing. Acknowledgment is made to the publishers who have allowed quotation from their works.

The editors thank all concerned from Dan Sillers who planned the conference, to Barrie Lind who typed and re-typed it, and Robert De Farges who printed it.

LOUIS SHORES
RORERT JORDAN
JOHN HARVEY

Easter, 1966

21.

LIBRARY-COLLEGE USA BIBLIOGRAPHY

ALONG THE WAY: A BIBLIOGRAPHIC CHECKLIST
Of Some of the Writings Relating to the Library-College Idea.

The seventy-one entries, alphabetically arranged are by no means all of the writings about Library-College. But they are most of the readings that have caught best my idea of the Library-College. I am sure there are many omissions, largely due to my failure to record as I read. Robert T. Jordan, in *The Library-College* (Drexel Press, 1966, Appendix D) and Sister Helen Sheehan in her fine *Library Trends* overview, have both contributed discriminating bibliographies.

Perhaps my colleagues in bibliography will forgive my experimenting with entry form, even if they will not overlook some deficiencies, which I am sure this checklist has. Principally, I have taken the good H. W. Wilson volume-page form and treated it as collation, *after* imprint. I have adopted the English teacher's title capitalization rather than our catalog card form. From a long life of reviewing and being reviewed I know that the idea can be subordinated to the form.

1. "The ACADEMIC LIBRARY as an Instrument of Learning: a symposium by a panel consisting of Harvie Branscomb, B. Lamar Johnson, Hilton C. Buley, Stafford North, John E. Tirrell, Woodburn O. Ross, Dan J. Sillers. *The Library-College Journal,* Fall, 1968.

2. BASKINS, Samuel, ed. *Higher Education: Some Newer Developments.* McGraw-Hill, 1965.

3. BERGEN, D. P. "Librarians and the Bi-Polarization of the Academic Enterprise." *College and Research Libraries,* 1963. 24:467-80.

4. BERGEN, D. P., ed. *The Library and the College Climate of Learning.* Syracuse University Schools of Library Science and Education, 1966.

5. BERGHOLZ, H. "Daniel George Norhof, Overlooked Recursor of Library Science." *Libri,* 1964. 14:44-50.

6. BESWICK, Norman. "Librarians and Tutor-Librarians." *The Library-College Journal,* Spring, 1969. 2:12.

7. ———————. "The 'Library-College'—the 'True University?'" *Library Association Record,* 1967. 69:198-202.

8. BRANSCOMB, Harvie. *Teaching With Books.* Chicago, American Library Association, 1940.

9. "CAMPUS '65." *Newsweek.* March 22, 1965. p. 43-63.

10. CARLYLE, Thomas. *On Heroes, Hero-Worship and the Heroic in History.* New York, Scribner, 1903.

11. CLAYTON, Howard. "Introducing the *Library-College Journal: a Magazine of Educational Innovation.*" *The Library-College Newsletter,* 1967. 16:2.

12. CONFERENCE OF EASTERN COLLEGE LIBRARIANS. *Library-instructional Integration of the College Level.* Chicago, ACRL, 1955.

13. DALE, Edgar. "The Teacher and Technology." *Education Digest,* 1964. 24:24-27.

14. DOBER, Richard P. *The New Campus in Britain: Ideas of Consequence for the United States.* New York, Educational Facilities Laboratories, 1965.

15. DREXEL LIBRARY-COLLEGE CONFERENCE (Philadelphia, 1966). "Proceedings." *Drexel Library Quarterly,* 1968. 4:1-2.

16. "ELECTRONIC LEARNING CENTER." *Catholic School Journal,* 1966. 66:32-33.

17. ELLSWORTH, Ralph E. *The School Library.* New York, Center for Applied Research in Education, Inc., 1965.

18. ———————. *The School Library; Facilities for Independent Study in the Secondary School.* New York, Educational Facilities Laboratories, 1963.

19. EURICH, Alvin C. "The Commitment to Experiment and Innovate in College Teaching." *Educational Record,* 1964. 45:49-50.

20. GARDNER, John W. "Education as a Way of Life." *Science,* 1965. 148:759-61.

21. GAYLOR, Robert. "The Philosophy of the Last Frontier." *The Library-College Journal,* Summer, 1969. 2:35-40.

22. GIVENS, Johnnie. "The Small and Medium-sized College Library." *Southeastern Librarian,* 1957. 7:12-15.

23. GORE, Daniel. "Anachronistic Wizard: the College Reference Librarian." *Library Journal.* 89:1688-92.

24. GOUDEAU, J. M., *et al. Impact of the Academic Library on the Educational Program.* Washington, D.C., U.S. Office of Education, 1967. (New Dimensions in Higher Education, no. 29.)

25. HATCH, Winslow R., ed. *Approach to Independent Study.* Washington, D.C., U.S. Office of Education, 1965.

26. HIRSCH, Felix E. "Uses of the Book Collection in the Teaching Program of a Progressive College." *College and Research Libraries II,* 1940.

27. HOLLY, James F. "Applications of the Library-College Approach to Macalester College." *Minnesota Libraries,* 1966. 21: 319-22.

28. HYMAN, L. W. "Advancing Education by Elimination of Classes." *Journal of Higher Education,* 1961. 32:213-15.

29. JOHNSON, B. Lamar. *Islands of Innovation Expanding Changes in the Community College.* New York, Glencol Press (Crowell, Collier, Macmillan, Inc.) 1969.

30. __________. *The Librarian and the Teacher in General Education.* Chicago, ALA, 1948.

31. __________. *Vitalizing a College Library.* Chicago, ALA, 1939.

32. JORDAN, Robert T., ed. "The College Talkshop, Kenyon College, June 24-29, 1962." (Mimeographed summary).

33. JORDAN, Robert T., *et al.* Impact of the Academic Library *on the Educational Program.* Washington, D. C., U.S.O.E., 1967.

34. __________. "The Term 'Library College,' Genealogy of the Idea: Theory, Practice and Publications." *The Library-College.* Philadelphia, Drexel Press, 1966, p. xxiii-xxv.

35. KNAPP, Patricia. *Independent Study and the Academic Library.* Washington, D.C., U.S.O.E., 1964.

36. __________. "Suggested Program of College Instruction in the Use of the Library." *Library Quarterly,* 1956.

37. ________. *The Monteith College Library Experiment.* New York, Scarecrow Press, 1966.

38. KROHN, Mildred L. "Study in Self-reliance—the Shaker Heights Learning Experiment." *Library Journal,* 1965. 40:4520-22.

39. KUHLMAN, A. F. "Can We Teach With Books?" *Southeastern Librarian,* 1957. 7:5-9.

40. LEUBA, Clarence. "Using Groups in Independent Study." Antioch College Reports, 1963. 5:2-4.

41. *Library-College Journal,* Library-College Associates, 1968.

42. *The Library-College Newsletter.* 1965-67. No. 1-18.

43. MAXFIELD, David K. *Counselor Librarianship: A New Departure.* Urbana, University of Illinois Library School, 1954.

44. MEIKLEJOHN, Alexander. *The Experimental College.* New York, Harper, 1932.

45. MINDER, Thomas. "Library Teaching—Engineering Model." Library-College. Philadelphia, Drexel Press, 1966.

46. MOUSOLITE, Peter S. "A Program for the Talented College Student." *School and Society.* 1966. 94:125-26.

47. ORNE, Jerrold. "An Experiment in Integrated Library Service." *College and Research Libraries,* 1955. 16:353-59.

48. OVERAGE, Carl F. J. *Intrex.* Cambridge, Mass., M.I.T. Press, 1965.

49. OXHANDLER, Eugene K. "Bringing the 'Dons' Up to Date." *Audio-Visual Instruction,* 1963. 8:566-59.

50. PATTERSON, Franklin. *The Making of a College.* Cambridge, M.I.T., 1966.

51. PERKINS, Ralph. *The Perspective Teacher's Knowledge of Library Fundamentals.* New York, Scarecrow Press, 1965.

52. POSTLETHWAIT, S. N., *et al. An Integrated Experience Approach to Learning, with Emphasis on Independent Study.* Minneapolis, Burgess, 1964.

53. ________. "Time for Microcourses." *The Library-College Journal,* Winter, 1969. 2:11-23.

54. Reading for an Age of Change Series. American Library Association, 1962.

55. RICHARDSON, Ernest C. "The Place of the Library in a University." *ALA Bulletin,* 1961. 10:8.

56. RUSH, N. Orwin. "The Library—The Focus of the Classroom." *Association of American Colleges Bulletin,* 1950.

57. SHEEHAN, Sister Helen. "The Library-College Idea: Trend of the Future?" *Library Trends,* 1969. 18:93-102.

58. SHORES, Louis. "Just Suppose . . ." *School Libraries,* 1964. 14:23-25.

59. ________________. "The Library Arts College, a Possibility in 1954?" *School and Society,* 1935. 41:110-14.

60. ________________. "The Library College Idea." *Library Journal,* 1966. 16:3871-5.

61. ________________. "The Library Junior College." *Jouior College Journal,* 1966. 36:6-9.

62. ________________. "The Undergraduate and His Library." (In *The Library in the University*: The University of Tennessee Library Lectures, 1949-1966; intro. by William H. Jessee; editor John David Marshall. Hamden, Conn., The Shoe String Press, Inc., 1967. p. 197-207.

63. SHORES, Louis, *et al. The Library-College.* Philadelphia, Drevel Press, 1966.

64. SINGER, Len. "Florida Atlantic University." *Audio-Visual Instruction,* 1963. 8:236-42.

65. SKINNER, B. F. "Why Teachers Fail." *Saturday Review,* 1965. 48:198-202.

66. SMITH, Robert E. *A Review of Published and Unpublished Material Concerning College and University Learning Resource Centers.* Champaign, Illinois, Richardson, Severns, Scheeler & Associates, 1965.

67. STICKLER, Hugh, ed. *Experimental Colleges.* Tallahassee, Florida State University, 1964.

68. STONE, C. Walter. *A Library Program for Columbia.* Pittsburgh, 1965.

69. TIDWELL, Roy. "The Oregon Plan." *Library Journal,* 1965. 90:3686-89.

70. TIRRELL, John E. "(Total!!) Independent Study at Oakland; Oakland Community College in Michigan Seeks to Develop a New Model." *Junior College Journal,* 1966. 36:21-23.

71. WILSON, Louis Round. *The Library in College Instruction.* New York, H. W. Wilson, 1951.

LIBRARY-COLLEGE USA

INDEX

SCHEELE MEMORIAL LIBRARY
3 6655 00001918 2
LB2364 .S55
Shores, Louis, 1904-/Library-c